REVIVE

LEADING CHANGE – IGNITING MOVEMENT

JIM STRECKER JR PhD

Revive: Leading Change – Igniting Movement

Copyright© 2025 Jim Strecker Jr

Cover design by Jim Strecker Jr
Cover photo by Paige Renzelman

Printed in the United States of America

DEDICATION

For Maegan, Mara, Asher, Devon, my parents, and
Irene – and all those who won't give up on the
church.

ABOUT THE COVER

The photo on the cover of this book is of the White River in Washington state. The source of the White River is the Emmons Glacier on Mount Rainier. The solid rock in the lower half of the photo represents the never-changing identity and mission of the Christian Church. The movement of the white water reflects two realities. First, the Christian Church exists in an ever-changing river of culture, requiring Christians to hold firm to the rock while embracing change to serve others' needs. Second, the always flowing movement of the water represents the Church as a movement, flowing from an ancient source to bring life to the world.

I thank Paige Renzelman for her care and for seeing the beauty of God's creation, and for sharing her passion and talent through her photography. Paige, you are in our hearts forever as we remember your kindness, laughter, and passion. We look forward to being with you again in the new kingdom.

I am thankful for the generosity of the Renzelman family, for their years of investment in my life, and always including me and my family in their disciplemaking way of life. I am grateful for your willingness to share Paige's legacy through the art for the cover of this book.

CONTENTS

INTRODUCTION

I believe in the local church. I believe the local church is God's plan "A" for bringing the good news that Jesus is Savior and King to the world. God has a mission. In his gospel account, John proclaims God's simple redemptive mission. "For God loved the world in this way: He gave his one and only Son, so that everyone who believes in him will not perish but have eternal life. For God did not send his Son into the world to condemn the world, but to save the world through him" (John 3:16-17). Jesus is God's plan A, and God's plan A includes the church. Yet, the portion of the Bride of Christ represented by Western churches and denominations in the United States is not flourishing. Sure, the Western church is surviving. New church plants start while other churches shut their doors. People surrender their lives to Jesus and begin following Him, while others walk away from church disillusions, disconnected, and disappointed. Others deconstruct their faith, dismissing sound doctrine and the value of participating in a local church. Every follower of Christ wants the Western church to do more than survive. We want the church to REVIVE!

I came to faith in Christ at the age of sixteen, in the mid-1980s, in a non-denominational church in the greater Seattle area. At the time, I didn't know the two-thousand-plus-year history of the church, what a denomination was, or why my home church was non-denominational. I knew that my youth pastor followed Jesus, and I wanted to follow Jesus, too. Cru and other parachurch ministries forged my youth pastor's ministry training. His ministry approach drove a missional purpose: Christians are supposed to tell others about the good news of Jesus. I quickly developed a passion for gospel-fueled mission and was surrounded by friends who helped me follow Jesus while we helped others find and follow Jesus.

Before it was cool, I was a computer nerd, so I didn't fit into the standard 1980s student cliques. One day, as I wrestled with living out my identity in Christ and what my gospel mission might look like beyond high school, I began praying for the other students in my computer programming class. In the middle of that prayer, God called me into full-time ministry. I shared my experience with my youth pastor, and he immediately invited me to become his shadow and learn about leading others. I went from computer nerd to Jesus-nerd. Our goal was to reach lost teens, disciple them, and launch them into God's mission locally and globally.

Throughout my years working with students in the context of local churches, the Holy Spirit launched some students into various vocations on gospel mission. Yet, others walked away from Christianity. Many, probably most, found themselves in between mission and mutiny. They attend church and identify as Christians. They genuinely care about others, and Christian values mark their lives with Jesus-like values such as kindness, generosity, and compassion for the poor. But the primary purpose driving their lives is not the mission of God, of proclaiming Jesus as Savior and King in their community and throughout the world. I might sound harsh in making such a judgment, but the truth is that we all struggle to keep God's mission as our priority. I struggle with keeping God's mission as my priority.

After three and a half decades of serving in local church student ministries, I returned to school. I hoped that I would help the church better reach and disciple students. However, as my research began, I quickly realized that the Western church struggled to make disciples of all ages, not just students. I began studying the church and leadership through an interdisciplinary approach, combining theology with sociology. I explored the effectiveness of churches, church organizational models, church leaders, and church leadership. I found that the current church measures for success assess institutional effectiveness but struggle to describe people transformed from death to life by Jesus. Jesus didn't begin an institution. Jesus began a movement. We cannot measure a movement as if it is an institution. If the Western church will revive, the way we lead the church must change.

How we lead matters. How we lead ourselves, our families, the community, and the local church matters. I am writing this book for followers of Jesus who are involved in any leadership level within the local church.

As leaders, we need to ask:

Is our church more like an institution or a movement?
What does it look like to lead in a local church successfully?
Why is a revived church important in our world?
What does it mean that the church is a movement?
What does it mean that the church must revive?
How do we lead change in the church?

What kind of leadership will it take to lead a revived church?

If the church must revive, where do we begin?

I hope that as you read this book, you will wrestle with these questions. My aim is to paint a vision for reviving the Western church. I want to captivate your heart with a vision for constructive change, helping every church engage in missional movement. The Church is God's plan A to proclaim Jesus as Savior and King throughout the world. God, we pray, REVIVE Your church!

You Can Read This Book in About 10 Minutes

Leaders, paid or volunteer, are busy. When you are busy, how you spend your time matters. That is why I included a special chapter at the end of this book. If you only read the last chapter. You will get the broad brushstrokes of the book. I wrote the last chapter, envisioning that we are riding an elevator down to a lobby. In the lobby, there is a coffee shop.

After brief introductions, you ask me what my thoughts are about the state of the Church and how we might help revive the Church as a disciplemaking movement. As the elevator descends, I intentionally limit my content, expressing my thoughts in a shortened elevator speech. My goal is that our time riding the elevator will encourage you to invest some of your valuable time, grab a cup of coffee, and sit with me as we share ideas and mutually revitalize one another's fire for God's mission and His movement, which we call the Church.

A ding sounds, indicating that the elevator is here. As the doors open, you can choose your own adventure. Clear your schedule and sit down for a cup of coffee, and we will embark on Chapter 1, or if your time is short, begin with Chapter 8.

CHAPTER 1

ON OUR WATCH

Jerusalem, I have appointed watchmen on your
walls; they will never be silent, day or night.
There is no rest for you, who remind the LORD. Do
not give him rest until he establishes and makes
Jerusalem the praise of the earth. The LORD has
sworn with his right hand and his strong arm: I
will no longer give your grain to your enemies for
food, and foreigners will not drink the new wine
for which you have labored.
Isaiah 62:6-7 (CSB)

Where there is no hope in the future, there is no
power in the present.
John Maxwell

The Covid-19 pandemic changed everything! As you read
that statement, the roll of your eyes further supports how
quickly we humans acclimate to a new normal. Not to
date myself too early in our conversation, but I was born
in the 1970s and raised in the 1980s. Learning to drive was
carefree in the mid-1980s; I could fill the tank on my VW
Bug (a Bug, not a New Beetle) with a few crumpled dollars

in my pocket. Ice cream cones at the were $.25, and a gallon of regular gasoline was under $.80. Fast forward just ten years, and I remember being frustrated because I was paying almost two dollars per gallon at the pump. Today, I am teaching my sixteen-year-old son the ins and outs of driving. When I was my son's age, the only thing special about our '69 VW Bug was the movie franchise starring number 53. The car had no fancy gadgets like cruise control or backup cameras. Let's be real: my heating and defrost system involved handing a 12-volt hairdryer and a towel to whoever was lucky enough to ride shotgun. As my sixteen-year-old pulls away from the curb, we get excited about paying under $3.50 a gallon instead of the $4.25 that ended my pickup truck driving days. Each day, everything is changing.

Change Isn't Always Bad

The good news? Humans adapt rapidly to change. The wiring in our brains intentionally transforms today's pleasurable or painful change into tomorrow's new normal. Major or minor changes to our lives becoming or feeling normal is called the hedonic treadmill[1]. As the world around us changes, the emotional acceptance of new circumstances changes from current discomfort to a future, happier state. In the past, I was content paying less than a dollar per gallon for gasoline. Now, I am paying three or more dollars a gallon, and I guess I'm content. Maybe I am just happy I'm not paying more. I grew up without a recollection of the gas prices of the early 1970s, so my sixteen-year-old self couldn't conceive of a world where gasoline is more than a dollar per gallon. Change is all

around us: good change and bad change. If you don't like
the change today, wait until tomorrow—according to the
hedonic treadmill, it might feel like the new normal.

But the new normal is the problem. When change
is good, the new normal is good. But when change is
bad, the new normal might feel good even if it's not. The
problem is perspective. When yesterday's change is today's
normal, we lose perspective, and it is difficult for us to
sense the presence and power of a problem. Immersed in
the problem, we don't even know we need distance to get a
different perspective.

Upon graduating high school, I wanted to follow
God's call and become a pastor. My perspective was
limited. I didn't have much church experience when I
started following Jesus, so my home church was the only
church model I knew. I was caught in a cultural bubble
fueled by what was normal to me. When I stepped into
youth/student ministry as a young leader, paid youth
workers or pastors were normal. Then, twenty years
later, in 2008, everything changed. A man who had lived
through the advent of parachurch youth ministry, church-
based youth ministry, and the era when it was normal
for churches to have youth pastors crafted a history of
youth ministry—a history I had never heard before. Mark
Oestreicher[2], in his book Youth Ministry 3.0, addresses
the rapid shifts in youth culture and how ministry to
students has, hasn't, or needs to change as culture changes.
Oestreicher's historical accounting focused on ministry to
students, inside and outside the local church. He identified
problems and potential mistakes, some of which still
influence youth ministry today. Oestricher's critique and

call for change offer a unique perspective for churches within Western culture in the global north. Therefore, as the pace of cultural change increases, leaders need to intentionally pursue perspective beyond their cultural bubble to avoid becoming caught in the undertow of the hedonic treadmill.

The Changing Now

Today, everything is different—or is it? In high school, I remember someone saying in a youth meeting that everyone thinks their generation is the worst and will be the last. Today, we deal with many divisive social problems, including hunger, poverty, homelessness, crime, disease, addiction, mental health, violence, abuse of power, racism, classism, slavery, terrorism, and war. In the middle of all these social problems, cultural views have shifted from valuing participation in a local church or embracing religious faith to finding reassurance, hope, and direction. Adding to the shifting culture is the polarization and divisiveness of social problems, leading some to craft a view of themselves and the world based on the loudest voices streaming and screaming across a digital landscape[3]. The loud voices often find their way into our lives through social media on our digital devices and the cell phones we carry everywhere.

The cell phone turned smart phone is a window into myriad worldviews for users who are mostly untrained to filter the good from the bad. Digital technology has provided many benefits to society, yet the new normal of digital technology has a cost. Anxiety has increased by over 20% since the advent of the smartphone, and empathy is

down. Smartphones are a window exposing our children
to cyberbullying, internet addiction, and pornography as
early as five years of age[4]. Surrounded by the problems
of Western culture, the Christian Church is struggling as
attendance declines and the surrounding culture does not
align, and at times rages against, the values taught in the
Bible. As Western culture continues to change, the new
normal is a devalued and marginalized Western church.

Yet, the descriptions of our current cultural
predicament (minus the digital technology) are familiar
to those of first-century Rome. Rodney Stark's[5] account in
The Rise of Christianity of Rome sheds light on hope for
today's Christian church. The early church came to life in
an oppositional culture. The values of Roman culture in the
first century differed dramatically from the values of the
early church. Yet, the church experienced vitality as Christ's
followers lived differently than those outside God's family.
The early church proved that light shines brightest in the
darkness (Philippians 2:15). It may be odd to find hope for
a new vitality or revitalization of the Western church in the
dire description of first-century or current Western cultures.
Still, where the church thrives, there is hope.

A Revitalization Movement

Stark describes the early church's efforts in fulfilling
the Great Commission, found in Matthew 28:16-20, as
a revitalization movement. A revitalization movement
is a collection of people working together to change the
practices and values of a society[6]. Disciplemaking and
revitalization synergistically link together through the
Matthew 28 Great Commission.

> The eleven disciples traveled to Galilee, to
> the mountain where Jesus had directed them.
> When they saw him, they worshiped, but some
> doubted. Jesus came near and said to them, "All
> authority has been given to me in heaven and
> on earth. Go, therefore, and make disciples of
> all nations, baptizing them in the name of the
> Father and of the Son and of the Holy Spirit,
> teaching them to observe everything I have
> commanded you. And remember, I am with you
> always, to the end of the age" (Matthew 28:16-
> 20, CSB).

Geoff Safford, pastor, speaker, church planter, trainer, and founder of the Light Company college ministry, memorably simplifies the revitalizing heart of Matthew 28:16-20: "Disciples who make disciples, that change culture." People make up culture. Change the people, change the culture. But isn't our focus as Christians just about the people and their salvation? Yes, but we cannot disconnect people from culture. People can allow culture to define them or choose to live in opposition to culture, but people cannot live without culture. Jesus transformed the lives of the early church, and they lived transformed lives as followers of Jesus in a hostile culture. The teachings and actions of the early church brought new life, or revitalization, to their culture. Changed people who love others, change culture.

Since before they were named, Christians have gathered as a collection of people committed to the redemption and restoration of those outside God's family

who don't know and follow Jesus. Disciplemaking is
what the Bible describes as introducing people to Jesus,
helping people identify as a part of God's family through
Baptism, and teaching them to live as followers of Jesus.
Disciplemaking changes people. People who are changed
change their culture because they love and live differently.
People changed by Jesus, in turn, care for the hurt,
oppressed, overlooked, and abandoned people. Christians
throughout history have a reputation for caring for the
widow, the orphan, the outcast, the cast aside, the poor, the
needy, the sick, those struggling with mental health, and
those treated as less than human. Christians drove cultural
change by establishing hospitals, orphanages, nursing care
facilities, music, and art galleries to promote and preserve
the beautiful, and labor unions to foster fair treatment and
the flourishing of communities[7].

Throughout history, the Church continues despite,
and possibly because of, its varied local expressions
consisting of different denominations, forms of gatherings,
styles of worship, language, preferred Bible translations,
and buildings or lack of buildings; one thing always
remains true: Jesus transforms lives. You could say that
Jesus revitalizes lives. Note: not a life, but lives! Looking
back through history, the early church looks like a
revitalization movement that transformed Roman culture.
A movement does not happen with just one person;
movement takes people. If the early church looks like a
revitalization movement, and we know that vitality, that
new life comes from Jesus, then we need to understand
what it means that the Church and all the little 'c' local

churches that make up the big "C" Church are, in fact, a movement.

Movement Perspective

For the Western church to revive, we need to understand the church as a movement. Christianity, or the Christian Church, comprises all followers of Jesus Christ. The scriptures describe the Church as the household of God (1 Timothy 3:14, Ephesians 2:19, 1 Peter 4:17), a family (Galatians 4:4-7, Romans 8:15-17), a body (Romans 12:4-5, Colossians 1:17-20, Ephesians 1:22-23, 1 Corinthians 12), a temple or dwelling place for God (Ephesians 2:22-23, 1 Peter 2:5), and a holy (1 Peter 2:5) or royal (1 Peter 2:9) priesthood. But does that make the Christian Church a movement? Recognizing Christianity or the Christian Church as a movement provides a new perspective on some of the Western church's problems. The Western church is losing people, influence, and opportunity. We know the church will prevail, Jesus promised (Matthew 16:18).

Talking about the church and movements might be negative for some, recalling news footage of protests like those addressing the Israel-Hamas conflict, which impacted many colleges and universities at the end of the 2023-24 school year. In Western culture, movements don't always mix with one's image of the church. Some social movements oppose the biblical values that represent the transformed life of a follower of Jesus. Mixing the concept of movement with the Church might even surface memories of Baptist church leaders and congregants protesting funerals, which earned them, and for some, Christians in general, the title of "hate group."

For others, the term movement fits comfortably with Christianity. Christianity has developed through the centuries, strengthened or divided by different movements. At one time, the papacy was a reforming movement in the church, and then the movement of the Reformation divided Roman Catholicism and Protestantism. The past century has seen mission movements, Bible study movements, holiness movements, house church movements, disciplemaking movements, and the Vineyard movement highlighted by Lionsgate Movies in 2023 and their movie The Jesus Revolution[8]. The church has a history of being a movement of movements.

A movement is a social phenomenon occurring when any group gathers and works together to make a change in a larger social context. The growing academic field studying the theories and applications of social movements may offer insight into the church as a movement. Social movement theory studies the life-cycle of movements—how they come together, organize, identify, mobilize, engage culture, and, in many cases, diminish[9]. Social movements center around the need for collective action and the purpose or mission of the group. The life-cycle of the Christian church almost mirrors a social movement. Rodney Stark identifies first-century Christianity and the first-century Church as a movement[5].

Stark's definition, focusing only on the outward effects of the first-century church, identifies the social benefits of Christianity but misses the redeeming and incarnational transformation that begins each time a person surrenders to Jesus. Jesus is our one true king and our only hope for redemption. Changing or revitalizing culture does not change people; the gospel of Jesus Christ transforms people, and living changed lives empowered by the Holy Spirit changes culture. A changed life is a significant apologetic, testifying that the gospel of Jesus Christ is good news. Therefore, Stark's definition adds to the spiritual and relational facets that define the church, which are derived from the scriptures rather than diminishing the scriptures. History reveals that the first-century church was more than a social phenomenon or a cultural change agent.

The prevailing view in theology (Acts 2) and academic literature is that Christian churches or congregations are characterized by gatherings of Christians, participation in teaching and worship, and observance of religious rituals and sacraments[10]. The portrait of the Christian Church painted by theology depicts the Church as a spiritual presence of worship and sacrament, God's actual household and dwelling place. Stark and other historians see the same Church from another angle as a beneficial community and cultural change agent. Theology argues that we must understand Christianity and the Church as more than a social phenomenon.   A prevailing theological and academic view of the church posited by Timothy Keller and others[11] suggests that the Christian church has a dual nature—divine and human—an invisible, supernatural, spiritual nature and a visible aspect comprised of organized gatherings of believers and their interaction with their community and culture. Viewing the church throughout history, Stark would agree with this prevailing combined theological and academic understanding of the church. However, Stark would add that there is more to Christianity and the Church. The Church is also a movement.

The 'also' is key! The church is not just a spiritual institution or a social-change organization. It is a spiritual institution with a divine purpose and mission. Adding mission to the combined divine and human understanding of the Church introduces the concept of movement and the need to understand and engage the church as a movement throughout history and within our unique time.

Movement Changes Everything

I have very sharp knives in my kitchen. My left index finger was in a splint for over a month. Not being able to move my finger meant I needed to learn how to do things differently. Opening doors, getting my keys out of my pocket, and even tying my shoes had to be done differently because I couldn't move my finger. My stiff finger began when I was scanning the book titles at my local thrift store three decades ago. I came across a book on Chinese cooking. I have always been interested in learning cooking techniques from around the world. I have tried handmade pasta and ravioli, traditional Chicken Kyiv wrapped in newspaper, Poulet au Chocolat (chicken in chocolate sauce), Chile Rellenos, Lamb Korma Curry, Hunan Beef, and Dim Sum. I did not have the money to travel, so I explored the globe through different cuisines.

The thrift store cookbook taught me that cooking is all about cutting. The substance of each bite is determined by how the chef cuts the ingredients. Knives are important, and with my sharp knife, I slipped, cutting off the tip of my left index finger. My concerns all focused on the cut on the tip of my finger wrapped in gauze and immobilized. After four weeks of not moving my finger, the cut had healed, but the joints became stiff and less flexible. Not moving my finger caused a greater injury than my poor knife skills. I didn't understand the power of movement.

Understanding the nature and power of movement changes how we engage with and lead the local church. Engaging the church as a movement informs our identity and affects our values and choices. Leading the local church as a movement requires us to answer core identity, opportunity, and missional engagement questions: why does this local church exist, why are these people gathered here, and why now? Successful movements drive toward identified change; churches should drive toward changed lives and those changed lives spreading the good news of Jesus Christ in their community and worldwide (Matthew 28:16-20, Acts 1:8-9). Attending, participating, and leading the church as a movement requires a different approach.

Success in a Movement

How success is defined changes when we embrace the movement nature of the church. In the history of the Western church, measures such as attendance, finances, volunteerism, buildings, assets, conversions, and baptisms frame most of the vision and success of the local church[12] [13]. However, traditional measures of success may not benefit the church as Western culture continues to change. Academia continues to refine the study of social movements, suggesting that we should view success as more than achieved outcomes[14]. Movements are successful when they mobilize people toward collective action.

Applying movement success to the church reframes successful churches as achieving a measure of traditional metrics and mobilizing people toward collective action in God's redemptive story.

Engaging a church using traditional measures of success means attending regularly, giving money, and serving. Engaging in a church as a movement impacts how you live day-to-day as a personal apologetic for the good news of Jesus and as an attendee representing your local church. Leading a church using traditional measures or metrics often looks like preparing a weekly lecture or sermon and leading teams or committees to maintain and monitor assets, buildings, budgets, and baptisms. The ministry of the church focuses on attracting and maintaining attendance numbers. Activities, events, or programs are successful if they improve the church's metrics—even if Jesus is never mentioned. Engaging and leading the church as a movement requires more than the traditional measures of success that have formed and informed Western church leadership and engagement.

Mobilizing a Movement

Over two hundred years ago, five students from Williams College gathered to discuss and pray about God's redemptive mission and unreached people who were not Christians living in Asia. Today, we know this gathering as the Haystack Prayer Meeting[15]. During their first meeting, the students, Samuel Mills, James Richards, Francis Robbins, Harvey Loomis, and Byram Green, took shelter from a storm under a haystack. The young men continued to meet, discuss, and pray at what became known as the

Haystack Prayer Meeting. One meeting or a small cluster of prayer meetings doesn't describe a movement. Truthfully, if these five young men only met, discussed, and prayed, we might not know about their meetings and the haystack story. However, their commitment to mobilizing people for God's mission birthed the Brethren denomination, The American Bible Society, and the ABCFM (American Board of Commissioners for Foreign Missions), which launched over 1200 missionaries in the following fifty years. We remember the Haystack Prayer Meetings because it was a mobilization movement, not because someone took attendance.

Another mobilizing movement erupted about one hundred years later, the SVM (Student Volunteer Movement). Robert Wilder was a young college student committed to mobilizing young adults in God's redemptive mission through foreign missions. Although the SVM doesn't exist today, its impact continues through its missional vision, not its organizational structure. The vision of the SVM was simple, "the evangelization of the world in this generation."[16] SVM built their collective identity through commitment cards and a clear vision. SVM launched over 20,000 young adults into the foreign mission field with one purpose: to see the world evangelized in their generation.

SVM defined its purpose or mission by focusing on mobilization toward action to achieve defined outcomes. While movement outcomes mirror traditional measures of the church, movement mobilization adds a new perspective linking church success to the mobilization of attendees. Recognizing the movement nature of the church changes how church success is defined. Because local churches are part of the movement of the Church, success is as dependent on mobilization as it is on the ministries drawing people to attend. Movement changes how we engage the local church and how we lead the church.

During Our Watch

During our watch, Western culture grows increasingly divided and divisive while also growing increasingly biblically illiterate. Only 5% of Western Christians believe the Bible shapes their lives[17]. On our watch, the number who identify as no-religion or 'nones' is greater than those who identify as Christian for the first time in the history of the United States[18]. Sure, people left during COVID-19 lockdowns, but many of them returned with somewhat spotty church attendance. The church, the institution that informed the United States as it formed, is voiceless. As I talk with pastors and Christians from around the country, the majority agree that something needs to change in how the Western church operates. If the Western Church and all its local churches remain on the current trajectory, what might happen on our watch if nothing changes?

But there is hope on our watch! Our older generations yearn for the transformation of culture by God and His Word. Our younger generations are hungry to participate in changing the world. Hope flourishes on our watch if we can hold onto the rich biblical and theological foundations that formed much of the Western church and grapple with and engage in the Church as a movement! Engaging in the church as a movement changes everything. People in a movement live differently than people who belong to an institution. Leaders who lead a movement lead differently than leaders of institutions. Christianity is always one generation from disappearing. What happens on our watch matters. Movement matters!

In the following pages, we will explore the importance of the Western Church as a movement. We will begin with Jesus and the movement He started two thousand years ago. Then, we will explore what movement means for local churches and those who follow Jesus. Finally, we will turn our focus to leadership and calling. How do we, as church leaders—elders, deacons, ministry leaders, volunteers, pastors, missionaries, and church planters embrace the centuries-old stream of movement we call the Church of the Living God? How can we mobilize those around us on God's mission each day? To answer these questions, we must consider how we lead others by exploring the concept of Shepherding Leadership. We will also revisit our approach to personal calling and provide a compelling vision for why the church must revive.

Embracing the church as a movement changes the game from surviving to thriving. The church as a movement gives new hope to all who God calls to lead local churches as many generations, cultures, and faith traditions are released and mobilized with God in His mission. We need to stop playing defense. We need to stop fearing if the church will survive. I do not doubt that the Western church will survive, even if it does not change. Jesus promised the church would survive, and John affirms the church will survive.

I know your works, that you are neither cold
nor hot. I wish that you were cold or hot. So,
because you are lukewarm and neither hot nor
cold, I am going to vomit you out of my mouth.
For you say, 'I'm rich; I have become wealthy
and need nothing,' and you don't realize that
you are wretched, pitiful, poor, blind, and naked
(Revelation 3:15-17).

As many as I love, I rebuke and discipline. So
be zealous and repent. See! I stand at the door
and knock. If anyone hears my voice and opens
the door, I will come in to him and eat with him,
and he with me.
(Revelation 3:19-20).

In Revelation 3:21, John describes a goal for the
church that is greater than mere survival. John describes a
church that thrives, a church that flourishes! However, there
is hope on our watch, because John's words in the next
verse are an invitation. "Let anyone who has ears to hear
listen to what the Spirit says to the churches" (Revelation
3:22, CSB). There is hope for the Western church. Our hope
is greater than mere survival. If we are to realize the hope of
a flourishing church, the church must revive!

CHAPTER 1 – END NOTES

1. Brickman, P., & Campbell, D. (1971). Hedonic relativism and planning the good society. In M. H. Appley (Ed.), Adaptation-level Theory: A Symposium (pp. 287–302). Academic Press.

2. Oestreicher, M. (2008). Youth Ministry 3.0: A Manifesto of Where We've Been, Where We Are & Where We Need to Go (First Edition). Zondervan.

3. Strecker, J. (2022, February 10). Pt. 2 Metamodernism: Where is the Truth? Movement Matters. https://jimstrecker.wixsite.com/movement-matters/post/3-things-the-most-resilient-people-do-every-day

4. Digital Futures Initiative. (2020). For Parents | Teach Your Kids Digital Citizenship. Digital Futures Initiative. https://www.dfinow.org/for-parents/

5. Stark, R. (1997). The Rise of Christianity: How the Obscure, Marginal Jesus Movement Became the Dominant Religious Force in the Western World in a Few Centuries. HarperSanFrancisco.

6. Conerly, T. R., Holmes, K., & Tamang, A. L. (2022). Introduction to sociology 3e. Independently published.

7. Schmidt, A. J. (2009). How Christianity changed the world. Zondervan.

8. Erwin, J., & McCorkle, B. (Directors). (2023, February 24). Jesus Revolution [Biography, Drama, History]. Kingdom Story Company, Lionsgate.

9. Jasper, J. M. (2010). Social movement theory today: Toward a theory of action? Sociology Compass, 4(11), 965–976. https://doi.org/10.1111/j.1751-9020.2010.00329.x

10. Grudem, W. A. (2020). Systematic theology: An introduction to biblical doctrine (2nd ed.). Zondervan Academic.

11. Keller, T., Chester, T., Montgomery, D., Cosper, M., & Hirsch, A. (2016). Serving a movement: Doing balanced, gospel-centered ministry in your city. Zondervan.

12. Hoyt, W. R. (2011). Effectiveness by the numbers: Counting what counts in the church. Abingdon Press.

13. Myers, P. K. (2017). Authentic leadership and its relationship to ministerial effectiveness among pastors in the church of the Nazarene [Doctor of Philosophy, Indiana Wesleyan University]. https://www.proquest.com/openview/687bff9c54aafa73c359c8443d4f4fbb/1?pq-origsite=gscholar&cbl=18750&diss=y

14. Einwohner, R. (2014, January 1). Failed Movements and Movement Failures. Mobilizing Ideas. https://mobilizingideas.wordpress.com/2014/01/01/failed-movements-and-movement-failures/

15. Braga, J. M. H., Kiley Hurst and Dana. (2023, June 14). Support for the Black Lives Matter Movement Has Dropped Considerably From Its Peak in 2020. Pew Research Center. https://www.pewresearch.org/social-

trends/2023/06/14/support-for-the-black-lives-matter-movement-has-dropped-considerably-from-its-peak-in-2020/

16.   Ministries, G. (2014, October 10). The History of the Haystack Prayer Meeting. Global Ministries. https://www.globalministries.org/the_history_of_the_haystack_pray_10_10_2014_112/

17.   Gary, J. (1986). The story of the Student Volunteer Movement. World Christian Magazine, July/August. https://campusministry.org/article/the-story-of-the-student-volunteer-movement

18. Burge, R. P. (2021). The nones: Where they came from, who they are, and where they are going. Fortress Press.

CHAPTER 2

WHY NOW?

But an hour is coming, and is now here, when the true worshipers will worship the Father in Spirit and in truth. Yes, the Father wants such people to worship him. God is Spirit, and those who worship him must worship in Spirit and in truth.
John 4:23-24 (CSB)

In the same way, the Church exists for nothing else but to draw men into Christ, to make them little Christs. If they are not doing that, all the cathedrals, clergy, missions, sermons, and even the Bible itself are simply a waste of time.
C.S. Lewis, Mere Christianity

Momentum Lost

Professional football teams invest significant time and money to assemble the most talented team each season. The goal is for their team to win. Win games and eventually win the Superbowl. Winning seasons begin long before the first snap. Coaches and scouts prospect tens of athletes, watch hundreds of games, and log thousands of hours watching videos. Scouting is an immense task to find a player with the right skill and talent for a position that will work with the team. Did you catch that? The player must work well with the team; they must add to the team's chemistry. Team chemistry is essential to playing well together.

Team chemistry is vital for synergy and key to group momentum. Synergy is simply getting more out of us than we offer by ourselves. Good players know and execute their positions on the team. Good teams work together, creating synergy among the players, leading to success, and creating momentum. But when the team doesn't work well together, they lose more than synergy; they lose momentum. One early February, I watched a big game between a team from Green Bay and a team from Denver. Each player on the field was a professional skilled at executing their roles on the team. As I watched the game, frustration replaced the excitement of a live sporting event. I was rooting for the team from Green Bay, but they had no synergy and no momentum. They lost. No surprise; winning without momentum is difficult.

American Christianity and the churches it represents in the United States are reaching a critical point. In 2021, Gallup reported an 80-year low in American's connection to religious institutions[1]. There are also reports of an increase in those who are irreligious or choose no religion[2]. The decline in church attendance doesn't mean every church is shrinking, but the trend reveals that most churches have a decreasing membership. Additionally, fewer young people are involved in church than in previous generations[3].

Aging congregations fuel this critical moment for the Christian church in the United States. Many Traditionalists remain active in church leadership. The Boomer generation, represented by many serving pastors and elders, began retiring in the early 2000s. Congregations and church leadership continue to grow older and less representative of their communities. Lifeway Research also notes that the younger generations are underrepresented among church attendees. The Christian church in the United States grows old while the church and culture diverge[5]. Like a worn-out and worn-down football team in the third quarter, the decreasing attendance, increased aging, and decreasing generational relevance suggest that churches may have lost momentum[3].

Then There was COVID-19

The United States changed dramatically after the attacks of September 11, 2001. Those old enough to remember remember where we were the moment the reality of the attacks hit. The loss of life, the destruction, the fear, the uncertainty, the heroes, and the stories all revealed the fragility of life. People awakened to their need for God, prayer, and community. Though it may have been short-lived, the American people remembered the importance of churches in our culture.

Most of us also remember March 2020, the beginning of the COVID-19 pandemic. We remember schools, businesses, restaurants, public gatherings, family gatherings, weddings, funerals, and weekly church services closing and canceling. Social distancing and digital communication became the norm as the world changed overnight. Remote learning, remote work, and remote worship became strategies for survival. Yet, as the government-induced restrictions in response to the pandemic lifted, many new habits formed during months or years of isolation, including not attending church, remained.

Post-COVID-19, it is no surprise that the Christian church in the United States is struggling. Social distancing in response to the pandemic only exacerbated the 20-year pattern of declining church attendance[3]. However, we may need to use caution when reading patterns of church decline since reported church attendance may be skewed by which Christian groups are counted or considered churches[6]. Yet, the record of the decline of the Christian church in the United States is well documented[3]. Ryan Burge, pastor and sociologist, affirms the church is in decline yet adds that amid the church's decline, the number of those who claim no faith in God is increasing[2].

Many church leaders are aware of declining numbers in general but feel helpless. The weekly ministry cycle keeps them between the growing needs within their congregations and the reality that the next Sunday is approaching. Some claim that everything is normal in the Christian church in the United States. Church growth theories of inaccurate measures among evangelical churches, premature reports of significant decline, and misrepresented decline due to population growth suggest the Christian church in the United States may be stronger than reported. However, it is common to hear of dwindling church attendance when meeting with pastors. We are at a cultural moment as the Christian church is taking moral lumps, and funerals seem to outnumber weddings. Momentum busters such as the increasing needs of church attendees, busyness, and struggling attendance and budgets may lead to feelings of helplessness and hopelessness.

Burge describes those not seeking religion as "Nones." The increase of the Nones in the 2018 GSS (General Social Survey) presents counterevidence to some overly optimistic theories of United States church decline[7]. The continuing rise of the Nones cuts through any misunderstanding concerning declining attendance in churches in the United States due to inaccurate measures[21]. The church in the United States has a history of measuring the attendance of Catholic and mainline Protestant churches while ignoring the attendance of smaller evangelical denominations and churches[6]. The Pew Research Center's 2025 Religious Landscape Study indicates that six Christians are leaving the church and their faith for every conversion to the Christian faith[21]. The increase of the Nones also addresses the assertion that the declining attendance of the church is simply the result of population growth exceeding the growth of church attendance. However, the increase in the Nones may support the idea that existing churches in the United States have limited or diminished effectiveness, resulting in decreased attendance.

The COVID-19 pandemic was a storm that the church in the United States could not avoid. Social distancing and government mandates closed many churches, and those remaining open were under extreme scrutiny from Christians and non-Christians alike. In the aftermath of the pandemic, attractional church models and church-health measures, which relied on attendance, giving, and program participation, were insufficient. Social distancing and the disruption of commerce in the

United States left many isolated, alone, in debt, and under-employed.

In direct contrast to the isolation during the pandemic, post-pandemic, people filled their calendars with family gatherings and outdoor activities, which now filled the time slot and priority once reserved for church. Many adults and youth despised the forced digital life, which consisted of online work and school. The convenience of online church services could not overcome the fact that it was online. Many waited for the pandemic to end, longing to attend church in person. As the pandemic restrictions began to lift, communities focused on getting students back in school and adults back to work, reconnecting with family and social groups. The busyness that ruled pre-pandemic culture was shunned[8] in response to lifting pandemic restrictions. Post-Covid, for some (if not many), doing less was still too busy, and their calendars seemed too full to consider returning to church.

The Institute for Family Studies reports that about 30% of practicing Christians did not return to church as the pandemic restrictions were lifted[9]. For those who did return, social distancing limited the number of attendees in a worship service. Post-COVID-19, churches face new issues, including fewer youth and older adults in worship. Still, many churches dealt with health concerns such as passing the offering plate, communion, and shaking hands. Even for the two-thirds of Christians who returned to church after the Covid-19 pandemic, the church was different. After the pandemic, the Christian Church in the United States has lost momentum.

Hit the Defrost

The winters in Minnesota are intense. Cold and snow arrive early to mid-fall and can stick around until late spring. During the cold, the ground freezes and freezes deep. In the Minneapolis metro area, it is not uncommon to have the ground freeze more than three feet deep. Cutting through the frozen ground to change the landscape of your backyard is nearly impossible. That is until late spring. The ice melts when the sun begins heating the ground, and the ground becomes workable again. The winter reality, all too familiar in the Northern Midwest, of freezing and melting applies to changing the organizational culture of churches[10].

A church's organizational culture comprises the church's theology, values, history, people, expectations, and how the church interacts with the outside community. Some churches may get stuck in a culture-rut with the intent of maintaining the status quo instead of helping people follow Jesus[10]. A church stuck in a culture-rut is a church that needs a culture change.

Changing the culture of any organization is difficult, especially when the culture is stuck or frozen. In the book Look Before You Lead: How to Discern and Shape Your Church Culture, Aubrey Malphurs recommends that any organization needs a melting experience before attempting significant culture change. Melting experiences can motivate churches to respond or act differently than normal. Melting experiences might include a building program, a capitol campaign, shutting church down for a Sunday to serve the community, an all-church prayer initiative, or a new hire. Malphurs's model suggests an opportunity for culture change following a melting event.

The Covid-19 pandemic hit the defrost for many churches. Pandemic restrictions forced churches to get out of the status quo or culture-rut and change. Churches and church leaders welcomed some changes resulting from the pandemic. Live streaming meant people did not have to miss church when they were ill or traveling. Pandemic restrictions also drove the need to learn digital communication among church leaders and attendees who may have been hesitant. However, not everyone welcomed the change. Many were forced to communicate digitally and responded by avoiding "doing church" online or "virtual youth group." The Covid-19 pandemic created an opportunity for culture change in the American church. Before we are frozen into a new status quo, now is the time to recapture God's vision for the church.

Getting Back to the Amazing Divine and Human Church

The movement of the Christian church describes a human institution and a spiritual community[11]. The Church is a human gathering where the Word of God is read and taught, God is worshipped, and people participate in sacraments[12]. When Jesus sent the Holy Spirit to his followers on earth, what we know as Pentecost, the Christian church was born. Yet, the church is not only a spiritual community. Early in the life of the church, we learn of general organization (Acts 2:42), resource sharing (Acts 5), and formal ministry structure (Acts 6). The movement of the early church was growing rapidly, creating new organizational infrastructure to meet the growing needs. While the church is an organized gathering of humans, the church is not simply a human institution.

Before Pentecost, the first mention of the church occurs in Matthew chapter 16. In Matthew 16:18, Jesus declares that he will build his church and that the gates of hell will not prevail against it. Matthew chapter 16 follows Jesus' disciples' struggle to understand the significance of the deceptive teaching of other religious leaders. It also precedes Jesus' chastising Peter for focusing on human priorities rather than God's. As the Gospel of Matthew scene unfolds, Jesus and his disciples may have been looking toward Caesarea Philippi with Mount Horeb in the background. Mount Horeb is the largest rock formation in Israel, home to fourteen pagan temples. Pagan worshippers carved niches into the limestone side of Mount Horeb, and pagan statues occupied each niche. Here, in the wilderness outside of Caesarea Philippi steeped in pagan worship, Jesus declares the foundation of his gathering, the church.

> Jesus responded, "Blessed are you, Simon, son of Jonah, because flesh and blood did not reveal this to you, but my Father in heaven. And I also say to you that you are Peter, and on this rock I will build my church, and the gates of Hades will not overpower it. I will give you the keys of the kingdom of heaven, and whatever you bind on earth will have been bound in heaven, and whatever you loose on earth will have been loosed in heaven." (Matthew 16:17-19, CBS)

The specific interpretation of Jesus' encounter with his disciples in Matthew's gospel remains debated. Did Jesus mean he would build his church on the testimony that Jesus is the Messiah, the Son of the living God? Or, as some suggest, that Jesus was referring to Peter as the very foundation and beginning of the church. What is not in debate is that the Christian church is Jesus' idea, and Jesus is the one who began the movement of the church and who builds his church.

Jesus asks his disciples what they and others believe about him. After providing a list of options that fall short of Jesus' real identity, Peter correctly identifies Jesus as the Messiah, the Son of God. Too often, we pass over this part of Peter's response and miss something very significant. So significant that Jesus brings it back up at the end of their conversation. In Matthew 16:20, Jesus warns the disciples not to tell anyone he is the Messiah. Jesus could have applauded Peter for paying attention and producing the correct answer. Instead, Jesus lays out three significant elements that are essential to the next phase of God's story—the part of the story we are in right now! Jesus's three elements—divine knowledge, community, and mission[13], are essential for any church. The elements, or movement markers, describe the church as a movement. A movement that will change the world.
Jesus begins by pointing to the source of Peter's answer— God. Divine truth is the first movement marker revealed in this passage. Divine truth is beyond common sense or mere observation. Peter's confession that Jesus is the long-awaited Jewish Messiah is revealed to him by God. Divine truth is central to the Christian faith and the foundation for every Christian and the church (John 6:44). Divine truth is found in God's Word, His revelation to us, and provides the core identity and purpose of the Christian and the Christian

church (Matthew 28:19-20). God's divine truth reveals God's story of loving and pursuing rebellious humanity and the story of Jesus, His life, death, resurrection, and ascension. Jesus declares that anyone who believes (John 3:16) is reconciled into a relationship with God. Each person may be saved; this is the good news of Jesus Christ! So, why build a church?

In the individualistic culture of the United States and the Western world, understanding salvation as a personal decision is natural. Jesus didn't simply declare that he would save people and reconcile them to God through the divine truth that elicited Peter's confession. Jesus declared that by his authority, he would also build his church, his assembly—his gathering. In declaring that Jesus will build his church, Jesus installs the second movement marker into the Christian church: community.

Jesus designed the movement community of the church to gather and mobilize[14]. Unlike the attractional models of the early 2000s, the mobilizing community of the church prioritizes gathering for the purpose of sending. Jesus declares that nothing, not even the Gates of Hell, a real place at the foot of Mount Horeb and the source of the Jordan River, will stop the mission of the Church. It is not until Matthew chapter 28 that we get a clear picture of God's mission, but by instilling purpose into his church, Jesus endows it with the third movement marker—purpose or mission. In one short interaction, Jesus reveals himself and his plans—Jesus designed his church as a movement.

As a spiritual institution and human organization, the Christian church is a mobilizing community. Jesus started the Christian church. Jesus is the founder and sustainer of the church. Jesus, one hundred percent God and one hundred percent human, created an organization that is one hundred percent spiritual and one hundred percent human. In the book of Acts, we find that the church was launched or empowered by the Holy Spirit and organized by humans filled with the Holy Spirit. There is nothing else like the Christian church. No other human organization or spiritual institution is one hundred percent spiritual and human. The Christian church, filled with humans, is sustained by Jesus and empowered by the Holy Spirit.

Historically and traditionally, churches regularly gather Christ's followers as a community for weekly worship services, small groups, and Bible studies. Traditional measures of church growth and effectiveness look at the church gathered. Measures of the church gathered assess elements including attendance, buildings, budgets, and ministries[15]. The gathering work of the church is essential. It encompasses disciplemaking, evangelism, healing, counseling, support, caring for one another, education, and training. Yet, the Christian church is more than a gathering of Christians; the church's design is to gather and send. Jesus instituted the community of Christians, the church, as a movement marker. The church, by biblical definition in Matthew 16, is a community that gathers to send; the Christian church is a mobilizing community for the movement of the kingdom of God.

Now is the Time

Has the Christian church in the United States lost momentum? Declining church attendance and diminished cultural impact might suggest the answer is yes. But can the spiritual and human community that Christ began and which is still empowered and mobilized by the Holy Spirit lose momentum? The Holy Spirit himself is the momentum of the church. Has the Western church lost momentum, or are the churches stuck in ruts focusing on the wrong measures of success? The COVID-19 pandemic completely muddled a model of success based on bodies, buildings, baptisms, and budgets. People's practices and priorities have changed. Western culture is in a crisis concerning relationships, addictions, and mental health. Will continuing self-help sermons, attractional ministry, and the shifting of Christians from one church to another benefit the movement of the Christian church or our communities? Has the Christian Church in the United States lost momentum?

Momentum is essential for a mobilizing community. From the inception of the Christian church, the Holy Spirit has been the church's momentum. Yet, momentum can be manufactured or squelched. Historians have chronicled the rise and fall of the movement of a local church[16]. The local church begins with high momentum and minimal organization. As the new local church is planted and begins to grow, increased organization is necessary. Eventually, as the church continues to grow, the church reaches an equilibrium between momentum and organization. Eventually, the organization exceeds the momentum. Once the organization exceeds momentum, the organization squelches momentum. Many churches seek to manufacture momentum through new programs, campaigns, or remodeling buildings to regain lost momentum. While

Western culture is still in flux following the global pandemic, now is the time for a new perspective.

The King and Perspective

King Solomon was the third king of Israel and the son of King David. He is known for being the wisest and wealthiest king and reigned in Israel for 40 years. Solomon is best known for expressing great faith in God by asking God for wisdom rather than riches or power. God gave him both. Solomon is also known as the king who built God a temple. Yet, over time, Solomon lost his perspective and his God-centered worldview. The result? Solomon made some life-changing mistakes.

> King Solomon loved many foreign women in addition to Pharaoh's daughter: Moabite, Ammonite, Edomite, Sidonian, and Hittite women from the nations about which the LORD had told the Israelites, "You must not intermarry with them, and they must not intermarry with you, because they will turn your heart away to follow their gods." Solomon was deeply attached to these women and in love. He had seven hundred wives who were princesses and three hundred who were concubines, and they turned his heart away. 1 Kings 11:1-3

Solomon was wise enough to understand the world's ways, and his relationship with God leads us to believe he maintained a God-centered worldview. A worldview that understood God's plan for shalom with God and the world. Yet, slowly, one choice at a time, Solomon drifted further from God. Solomon's changing worldview created a growing divide between choices that seemed best for Solomon versus obedience to God. God blessed Solomon; he was given riches and wisdom, he built the first Jewish temple, and God appeared to him twice. God specifically commanded Solomon not to pursue other gods. Somehow, the wisest person alive and writer of the book of Ecclesiastes adopted a worldview that separated his spiritual life from life in this world. Solomon began to live by his own understanding rather than God's wisdom. He gave his heart and his way of life to his wives and worshipped other gods.

Perspective

The perspective of three thousand years of history provides insight into King Solomon's successes and failures. Did Solomon have the perspective to understand that when he did what he did (turn his heart away from God and toward other gods), he got what he got (loss of God's protection and a divided kingdom)? Did Solomon blame others, his advisors, or his leadership skills? Today, we have a benefit over Solomon: time and distance. Yet, we lack time and distance when confronted with the diminishing Christian church in the United States. Do we, like Solomon, blame others, the culture, our predecessors, or our leadership skills?

Estimating the number of Christian denominations and sects in the United States is difficult due to the opening and closing of churches and the nebulous definition of a denomination. Rough estimates identify over 300,000 churches, and the number of denominations ranges from the hundreds to the thousands[17]. Despite the number of churches and denominations, there is significant concern that the Christian church in the United States is diminishing. If the Christian church is diminishing, are we missing something? Access to tools once reserved for elite seminarians now fuels the theological understanding of pastors and parishioners alike. Livestreams, podcasts, books, audiobooks, blogs, and social media feeds flood the landscape for church leaders. Yet, our churches are shrinking. How might we gain the needed perspective to address any concerns?

Was Solomon a Frog?

There is an old fable that has circulated Christian youth groups for decades. The tale of the frog and the kettle. In this non-scientific, fictitious story, frogs are placed into two different pots. The first pot contains boiling water. The frog immediately jumps out as it hits the water in the first pot. The quick actions of the frog save its life. The second pot is filled with cool water. The frog placed in the pot with cool water remains in the pot. Next, the frog-filled cool water pot is placed on a burner and slowly heated. Being cold-blooded, the frog doesn't notice the water temperature increase to a temperature that kills the frog. It is a fable of a constant hedonic treadmill.

The fictitious fable of the frog in the kettle explains how real humans can react with indignance when faced with an obvious injustice—about God or others. The frog jumps out of the boiling water to avoid harm. Yet, when the water is slowly heated, the frog remains until it dies. Likewise, humans may allow small sins or injustices to go unnoticed and accumulate over time, eventually causing significant damage. Solomon didn't marry hundreds of wives because he reasoned they would introduce him to false gods he could worship. Solomon, like many of us, would have reacted harshly if a foreigner told him he needed to worship Molech (a false god of the Ammonites who was worshiped through child sacrifice). However, as a loving husband, Solomon began by allowing his wives to worship their gods, helped them create places to worship their gods, and eventually joined in worshipping false gods (1 Kings 11:6-8).

Has the Christian church in the United States been affected like the frog in the warming water or Solomon with his many wives? Over time, has Western culture, specifically the culture and values of the United States, affected the Christian church? In this era in which the church has a diminished impact on the surrounding culture, has the surrounding culture impacted the church? Are churchgoers worried more about their place in society, their friend groups, or their retirement years than the lives of those who don't know Jesus? Is there an urgency for God's mission among the churches? Or will our generations allow history to patiently provide the perspective—the time and distance—needed to accurately view problems facing us now? Church leaders need a new lens for assessing the concerns facing the church.

A Different Vantage Point

One hundred years from now, history may provide a
clear view of the diminishing attendance currently faced
by the Christian church in the United States. Christians
in the United States are part of what scholars and
missiologists refer to as the Global North[18]. There is a trend
of Christianity moving away from the Global North to the
Global South. The time of Christian flourishing may be
over in the global north. Tina Zurlo, Todd Johnson, and
Peter Crossing provide a different vantage point offering a
predictive model of the growth of the Christian church in
the Global South and the decline of the Christian church
in the Global North. What is this different vantage point?
Combining information from various disciplines, including
missiology, religion, political science, and sociology, creates
a different lens through which to understand the growth
and decline of the church. Hindsight may provide the
clearest picture of what is happening in the Global North,
but a new perspective may help see and understand
the Western church differently. Learning from different
disciplines creates a different vantage point, which might
provide a fresh understanding of what is happening to the
church now.

One useful vantage point is called socio-theology.
Socio-theology may be useful in addressing issues
concerning the Christian church in the United States.
Combining sociology and religion, or theology, makes sense
since the disciplines work together, and there is growing
interdisciplinary support among scholars[19]. In a basic sense,
humanity and the church are deeply theological. Humans
are created in the *Imago Dei* (image of God) for God

(Ephesians 2:10), and the church is started, held together, and led by Jesus himself (Colossians 1:16-18). Theology helps us understand the identity, belonging, and purpose of humanity and the church[20]. Sociology helps us understand how humans and institutions behave and interact. A combined approach of sociology and theology may best inform our understanding of the issues facing the Christian church in the United States.

Embracing the divine and human, or theological and sociological, natures of the church may give us a path to move forward. The need for a new perspective, a new approach, has been rumbling for some time now. You can hear it in the lyrics from Keith Green to Rich Mullins and Andrew Peterson. The rumblings of a need to look at the church differently can be found in blogs and podcasts ranging from NT Wright to the Gospel Coalition. A groundswell of authors such as Leonard Sweet, Alan Hirsch, Aubrey Malphurs, and Will Mancini address the church and the writings of Skye Jethani, Bill Hull, Rebecca McLaughlin, and Kevin DeYoung seek to help Christians flourish in their church communities and their culture. In the constantly changing Western culture, the Christian Church is struggling. We need to gain a new perspective, see the church as fully divine and human, and allow our new perspective to revitalize our approach.

Now is the time for a different approach. The current trends of Western culture and the Covid-19 pandemic disrupted our ruts. The culture of the status quo is melted. Now is the time to take a fresh look at where the Christian church has come from and where God is leading us in the days ahead. God is raising multiple

voices from various churches and theological traditions to
call the Christian church to get out of its ruts and engage
the world incarnationally. Has the Christian church in the
United States lost momentum? Yes. But the game isn't
over yet! Even as I wrote this chapter, a revival of worship
and prayer erupted at Asbury College. And this revival
continues to spread among a generation desperately
seeking the truth. I pray that their search will lead them
into the open arms of Jesus—God is on the move!

CHAPTER 2 – END NOTES

1. Jones, J. (2021, March 29). *U.S. Church Membership Falls Below Majority for First Time*. Gallup.Com. https://news.gallup.com/poll/341963/church-membership-falls-below-majority-first-time.aspx

2. Burge, R. P. (2021). *The nones: Where they came from, who they are, and where they are going*. Fortress Press.

3. Foster, D. C. (2022). *The Post Covid Church*. Webb Publishing.

4. Earls, A. (2023, June 15). *Reversing the Shrinking Share of Americans Who Regularly Attend Church*. Lifeway Research. https://research.lifeway.com/2023/06/15/reversing-the-shrinking-share-of-americans-who-regularly-attend-church/

5. Keller, T. (2022). *The Decline & Renewal of the American Church* (Gospel In Life) [White Paper]. https://quarterly.gospelinlife.com/decline-and-renewal-of-the-american-church-extended/

6. Finke, R., & Stark, R. (2005). *The Churching of America, 1776-2005: Winners and losers in our religious economy* (Revised edition). Rutgers University Press.

7. Smith, T., Davern, M., Freese, J., & Morgan, S. (2019). *General social surveys, 1972-2018: Cumulative codebook / principal investigator, Tom W. Smith; co-principal investigators, Michael Davern, Jeremy Freese and Stephen L. Morgan*. (No. 25, p. 3,758). NORC. www.gss.norc.org

8. Hoch, M. (2022). The Postpandemic Pedagogue. *Journal of Singing*, *78*(4), 483–489.

9. Wang, W. (n.d.). *Number 2 in 2022: The Decline in Church Attendance in COVID America*. Institute for Family Studies. Retrieved February 16, 2023, from https://ifstudies.org/blog/number-2-in-2022-the-decline-in-church-attendance-in-covid-america

10. Malphurs, A. (2013). *Look before you lead: How to discern and shape your church culture*. Baker Books.

11. Keller, T., Chester, T., Montgomery, D., Cosper, M., & Hirsch, A. (2016). *Serving a movement: Doing balanced, gospel-centered ministry in your city*. Zondervan.

12. Grudem, W. A. (2020). *Systematic theology: An introduction to biblical doctrine* (2nd ed.). Zondervan Academic.

13. Cole, N. (2005). *Organic church: Growing faith where life happens* (1st edition). Jossey-Bass.

14. Leffel, G. P. (2007). *Faith seeking action: Mission, social movements, and the Church in motion*. Scarecrow Press.

15. Mancini, W., & Hartman, C. (2020). *Future church: Seven laws of real church growth*. Baker Books.

16. Addison, S., & Stetzer, E. (2012). *What Jesus started: Joining the movement, changing the world* (Illustrated edition). IVP Books.

17. Hartford Institute for Religion Research. (n.d.). *Fast Facts about American Religion*. Fast Facts about American Religion. Retrieved March 20, 2023, from http://hirr.hartsem.edu/research/fastfacts/fast_facts.html#denom

18. Zurlo, G. A., Johnson, T. M., & Crossing, P. F. (2020). World Christianity and Mission 2020: Ongoing Shift to the Global South. *International Bulletin of Mission Research*, *44*(1), 8–19. https://doi.org/10.1177/2396939319880074

19. Juergensmeyer, M. (2013). The Sociotheological Turn. *Journal of the American Academy of Religion*, *81*(4), 939–948. https://doi.org/10.1093/jaarel/lft049

20. Powell, K., & Griffin, B. M. (2021). *3 big questions that change every teenager: Making the most of your conversations and connections*. Baker Books.

21. Smith, G., Cooperman, A., Alper, B., Mohamed, B., Rotolo, C., Tevington, P., Nortey, J., Kallo, A., Diamont, J., & Fahmy, D. (2025). *Decline of christianity in the U.S. has slowed, may have leveled off*. https://www.pewresearch.org/religion/2025/02/26/decline-of-christianity-in-the-us-has-slowed-may-have-leveled-off/

CHAPTER 3

JESUS' MOVEMENT

Now the one sown among the thorns—this is one
who hears the word, but the worries of this age
and the deceitfulness of wealth choke the word,
and it becomes unfruitful. But the one sown on
the good ground—this is one who hears and
understands the word, who does produce fruit and
yields: some a hundred, some sixty, some thirty
times what was sown."
Matthew 13:22-23 (CSB)

Jesus died for our sins not so that we could sort
out abstract ideas, but so that we, having been
put right, could become part of God's plan to put
his whole world right. That is how the revolution
works.
N.T. Wright, The Day the Revolution Began

Jesus and Movement

Before Christianity, there was Jesus. Jesus—the historical,
religious, and political figure known in sacred and non-
sacred texts. For over two thousand years, people have been
talking about Jesus, writing about Jesus, learning about

Jesus, and teaching about Jesus. Who was Jesus, why did he live, how did he die? Does a two-millennia-old religious teacher matter in our world today? During the short thirty-three years between Jesus' birth and death, he became known as a good moral teacher among the Hebrews. Today, many cultures and faiths still regard Jesus as a good moral teacher. The first-century appeal of Jesus was far-reaching; crowds of Hebrews and non-Hebrews chose to follow Jesus. Jesus' followers formed an eclectic group; some were like Jesus, some were different from Jesus, Hebrew, non-Hebrew, rich, poor, educated, uneducated, powerful, and powerless. What was Jesus starting?

On the hills of the Judean countryside, crowds formed around Jesus. Some thought Jesus to be a religious figure, a teacher, or even a Hebrew rabbi. Others saw Jesus only as a potential political ruler, a leader, or a king. Still, others followed Jesus because he gave them food, helped people experiencing poverty, and healed those sick or disabled. Some may have followed because Jesus treated everyone with dignity and respect—especially those cast aside by the majority culture. Jesus did not merely tolerate people; Jesus spoke and acted in love towards everyone (Matthew 8:14-16; Matthew 15:21-27).

In the years following Jesus' death, Christians continued living out and mirroring the teachings and actions of Jesus. The early Christian church embraced the life and teachings of Jesus. The Church was a radical force within their culture. In the first-century culture, women, children, infants, enslaved people, people with disabilities, the infirm, and foreigners were often overlooked, discarded, and often considered and treated as less than human. However, Christians lived differently within their surrounding culture in a way that honored Jesus as their king. The worldview and approach to life found in the Christian Church testified to the life and freedom found only in Jesus. The living testimony of the early church brought about constructive changes in the surrounding cultures and resulted in changed lives. The cultural changes benefited the lives of those who surrendered to Jesus and the lives of those who did not.

Historian Rodney Stark defines the rise of Christianity in the Roman Empire as a revitalization movement[1]. Stark contrasts early Christians' actions against the norms of the Roman culture, noting that Christians welcomed people of all ethnicities, valued the sacredness of all life, valued women and children, and cared for those in poverty and crisis. Stark describes first-century Christians as teaching a renewed version of the Roman concept of peace with the gods, *pax deorum*, introducing the *new* reality that God loves humanity and made way for peace through Jesus Christ. God's story of His redemptive pursuit of rebellious humanity climaxed through Jesus' life, teaching, actions, death, resurrection, and ascension. Through his death on the cross, Jesus became the victorious conquering King, defeating sin, death, and the powers of darkness. Jesus did more than win a victory; he did more than win THE victory; Jesus had started something. Jesus had started a movement, but what kind of movement?

Movement DNA

Cadre Ministries, located in the upper Mid-West, partners with missionaries, pastors, churches, church leaders, and anyone willing to engage in Jesus' disciplemaking movement. Cadre Ministries operates within the larger movement of the Christian Church. Without discriminating against denominations, Cadre's team trains and mobilizes church attendees and leadership to live and promote Jesus' disciplemaking movement in their local churches. Cadre Ministries is an infusion of movement DNA spurring Jesus' disciplemaking movement in local churches. They gather like-minded Christians from across various churches into learning communities. These learning communities explore, reinforce, and provide accountability to employ the teachings and practices of disciplemaking. Through their efforts, the Cadre Ministries team has significantly impacted the Kingdom of God, infusing movement DNA into individuals, churches, and entire denominations. Cadre Ministries' impact reveals the need to invest in movement DNA to fuel and mobilize people on God's mission.

The National Cancer Institute defines DNA as the genetic material necessary for an organism to grow, organize, function, and pass on its purpose from one generation to the next. An organization's or church's DNA has become a descriptive metaphor for organizational culture, feel, personality, characteristics, values, ethos, purpose, mission, structure, and motivation. The metaphor of organizational DNA is prolific in discussions on churches and church leadership. Human DNA is complex. Church DNA is also multifaceted and can seem complex. However, movement DNA is basic, making engaging in movement and leading change within the local church accessible to every church leader and follower of Jesus.

How does the metaphor of DNA relate to movement? The DNA of the body consists of information, organization, and directions for the body to grow. The body's DNA is constantly reminding, uniting, instructing, correcting, and motivating the body to grow and fulfill its mission of being human. The DNA of movement, or what I will call movement DNA, defines and empowers a movement. Therefore, movement DNA is the needed information, organization, direction, and motivation to accomplish the mission of a group or a church. Did Jesus have movement DNA?

Neil Cole suggests a church's DNA consists of divine truth, community, and mission or purpose.3 The DNA of the Christian church consists of our connection with God, our connection with one another, and our commitment to God's mission, incarnationally engaging the world with the gospel of Jesus Christ. Missio-ecclesiology describes the relationship between the church and God's mission for the church revealed in the Great Commission (Matthew 28:16-20). Research working with the concept of missio-ecclesiology has identified three movement markers—connecting with God and His mission, connecting in a community that fosters missional accountability, and intentionally living on mission with God and others. The movement markers reflect the core elements of a social movement—purpose, mobilizing community, and social engagement.

So, did Jesus have movement DNA? The quick answer is yes! We can see each movement marker in Jesus' life, ministry, and followers. We see the movement marker of connection with God through Jesus' intimate connection

with God (John 10:30). Jesus sends the Holy Spirit so that
we, his church, would have an intimate connection with
Jesus and God (John 17:21). Jesus also connected with
others forming community, noting the second movement
marker. Jesus participates in a wedding (John 2), showing
his connections with family, friends, and the local
community. Jesus gathers and eats with his followers (Mark
2). Jesus chose twelve men to follow him closely (Luke 6)
and be his friends. John 17:21 also describes the intense
unity between Jesus and God, between Christians and Jesus
and God, and between fellow Christians. Finally, we see
the third movement marker through Jesus' commitment
to God's mission. Jesus describes and owns his purpose or
mission, which is to restore biblical justice (Luke 4:18-21), to
promote the presence of the kingdom of God (Luke 17:21),
and to accomplish the redemption of sinful humanity (Luke
19:10, Romans 8:3).

Jesus operated with the DNA of a movement.
Jesus passes these movement markers on to his followers,
the church. In Matthew 28:19-20, Jesus commands his
followers to go to everyone—all nations, tribes, tongues,
races, classes, and cultures. As Jesus' followers go, they
are to help people connect with God and live according to
who God is and to live as true humans, disciples of Jesus
living according to God's design. Jesus also commands his
followers to create a connected community among these
disciples through baptism. At its core, baptism indicates
belonging and commitment to the Christian community.
Finally, Jesus commands his followers to engage in the
ongoing multiplication of disciples through teaching and
training in Jesus' way of life. The movement markers reveal

that movement was Jesus' model for His church and central
to the story of Jesus' followers.

Movement Markers
When Jesus revealed the blueprints for his church
theologically, he described it using three essential elements:
divine knowledge, community, and mission. Through
studying the nature of churches and using the illustration
of DNA, Robert Cole identifies a church's essential DNA
as divine truth, nurturing relationships, and apostolic
mission[3]. While more goes into the ingredients of a
local church, these are necessary elements for a church's
biblical identity, purpose, and ability to engage in church
multiplication. Ecclesia-motus is an evidence-based
framework developed through a sociological study of
Western evangelical churches. Ecclesia-motus identifies
three elements needed for the church as a movement:
connection with God and His mission, community and
missional encouragement, and missional living[5]. The paths
of theology, church studies, and sociology lead to the same
address. The essential elements of the church describe the
church as a movement.

Connection with God and mission, a community
that encourages one another toward mobilization, and
living on mission comprise the essential movement markers
of the Christian church. Since everyone has DNA, the
illustration of DNA highlights that every church should
have these movement markers, even if they are ignored,
underrepresented, or repressed. However, DNA is overly
complex, with about three billion base pairs in the human
genome. The movement markers Jesus instilled into

the church are simple and can provide a pathway for church leadership, Christian engagement, and church revitalization. However, the church was not designed with movement markers only to be a movement. The church is a unique movement designed to transform people and change the world through the person and power of Jesus Christ.

The Impact of the Jesus' Movement

Christianity began as a movement. From the earliest days of the Christian movement, its members were known for radical religious views[6], counter-cultural social activism, and claiming to belong to a new king and kingdom[7]. Christianity worked to improve the value and dignity of women, children, and marginalized individuals. The movement of Christianity has produced orphanages, hospitals, fair labor standards, the abolition of the slave trade in England, equality for women, and the civil rights movement in the United States[8]. From a spiritual perspective, the message of Christianity has been transforming people eternally. From a social perspective, Christianity has been in tension with and transforming cultures around the world.

Christianity began under Jesus' radical leadership. Jesus' leadership and teaching are accessible and applicable independent of class, race, gender, or culture. Because Jesus' message and teaching are supra-cultural and accessible to all genders, ethnicities, and classes, the movement of Christianity produces collateral transformation. People near the gatherings of Jesus' followers benefit from the missional engagement of Christians. The Christian movement, begun by Jesus, has influenced art and architecture, liberty and law, volunteerism, and care for the vulnerable.

Christianity is a movement of movements. What kind of movement is Christianity? Is Christianity primarily a religious movement? Or is Christianity a social movement or a political movement? Christianity is one of the world's major religions, so it may seem obvious that, since Christianity is a movement, it is a religious movement. Jesus' self-declaration of deity (John 10:30) affirms Christianity's religious nature but does not limit the impact of Jesus' teachings, message, and followers to the boundaries of only a religious movement.

The Christian New Testament references the religious nature of Jesus' activity and purpose—including his death and resurrection. A basic definition of religion is humanity's attempts to relate to the divine. Jesus claimed he was divine and the only way for humanity to relate to God (John 14:6). Jesus placed himself at the center of religion as the divine that relates to humanity. Jesus turned human religion upside down, announcing that God is reconciling humans to Himself (2 Corinthians 5:19). Jesus' life, death, resurrection, and ascension activated God's redemptive plan to restore humanity to Himself, superseding humanity's efforts to relate to the divine. Jesus remains one of history's most significant religious figures two centuries later. Therefore, defining Christianity as a religious movement is reasonable.

However, could Christianity be understood as a political movement? Jesus himself spoke often about the kingdom of God (Mark 1:15) and that he is a king (John 18:37). Paul, in his letter to the church in Philippi, also declares that Jesus has authority to rule (Philippians 2:6-11). However, Paul also argues in Romans that Christians living counter to and in tension with the primary culture are to respect and submit to governing authorities.

Political movements mainly focus on changing the government to ensure that the treatment of the governed facilitates dignity and respect and that the marginalized have a voice and responsibility in relationships[9]. Some political movements are revolutions, as one group takes political authority and power from another. Other political movements are reformations or revitalizations, working within social and legal systems toward greater justice for the people. With two thousand years of Christians creating, reforming, and revitalizing governments worldwide, Christianity as a movement has helped increase dignity, respect, advocacy, and the responsible use of governmental power. Given the political impact of Christians through the centuries, evidence affirms Christianity as a political movement. Some present the concept of Christianity as a political movement, arguing for the need to understand the political sphere as encompassing both human and spiritual realms[10]. In *How God Became King*, N.T. Wright suggests that politically, Christians should live under God alone as King[11]. Wright's call for a pure theocracy runs counterintuitive to the movement nature of Christianity. The scripture promises that Jesus will reign and God will be the King when the new Heaven and Earth are complete. Until then, the movement of Christianity exists within and in tension with the human governments of this age. While Jesus' movement informs and involves the political sphere, it may be most helpful to understand Christianity as a political movement grounded in a kingdom above or beyond human governments, as Jesus said, "My kingdom is not of this world" (John 18:36).

Christianity makes sense as a religious movement and a spiritual-political movement. However, might Christianity be better understood as a social movement? Social movements encompass various types, including religious, political (reform and revolutionary), self-help, and reactionary movements[12]. Nevertheless, social movements are not a catch-all for all other movements. They have focused purposes that aim to address societal problems affecting groups of people constructively.

Social Movement and the Church

So, what makes a social movement a social movement? The literature broadly defines social movements as groups working toward a common goal centered on social change[12]. Social movements occur anytime people are united around a commonly identified need and seek to address that need for the benefit of others constructively. The definition of a social movement has three parts. First, people gather around a cause so that the cause and gathering inform the group's identity. Second, people gather in groups, reinforcing the larger group identity and informing individual purpose. Third, individuals and groups take action to fulfill the cause's goals. A social movement organizes people with identity, purpose, and action.

In response to the Israel-Hamas conflict that erupted in 2023, students protested violence done to Palestinian civilians and for humanitarian help for those experiencing violence. The response was positive and negative. Student protests positively raised public awareness of the plight of Palestinians. Negatively, some protests involved violence, disrupting academic classes and impacting colleges and universities, local governments, and law enforcement. Unfortunately, the positive and negative outcomes of the protests impacted the public's understanding of a social movement.

In the early 2020s, the United States experienced a growing number of social movements targeting climate change, employee treatment, racial discrimination, gender discrimination, and the rights and acceptance of the LGBTQIA+ community. For many, separating the concept of social movements from the goal of individual social movements is difficult. In these cases, the phrase "social movement" is equated with the subject or goal of the movement. The difference between a social movement and a social movement's goal is like the difference between gardening and growing tomatoes. Gardening defines the basic task of intentionally growing a variety of plants, which may include tomatoes. Growing tomatoes, however, defines gardening as producing tomatoes. Social movements describe the general mechanism of intentionally increasing justice in the world. However, when properly aimed at a specific area of injustice, a social movement informs identity, purpose, and actions, which mobilize people to make constructive change. Social movements can be a powerful tool to produce unity and constructive collective action to address specific needs or inequalities within society and culture.

The four gospel accounts in the New Testament paint two unique stories of Jesus. One story follows God's redemptive plan, redeeming rebellious humanity through Jesus' life, death, resurrection, and ascension. The second story illustrates what life is like when one lives within the kingdom of God with Jesus as their king. The first is spiritual, focusing on how God and humans can live together. The second story of the kingdom is sociological, focusing on how humans live with God and each other under Jesus' reign. Jesus' purpose in the kingdom story (Luke 4:16-30) of bringing good news to the poor and freedom to captive and oppressed people aligns with the purposes of most social movements. As we read the accounts of Jesus' life, we see Jesus furthering his kingdom view of life or his societal or social agenda through caring for the poor and healing the sick and blind. Jesus began the movement that birthed Christianity. Christianity started as a movement that revitalized broken human culture[13], and Christianity is still a movement today[14]. The four gospel accounts bring the spiritual and kingdom stories together in a now-but-not-yet tension of being saved and growing in our sanctification and Jesus being king. Jesus' followers live for kingdom purposes within broken human societies.

The movement of Christianity includes but is not limited to religious, political, and social movements. The movement of Christianity is about awakening followers of Jesus to live within human culture and society, yet surrendering to Jesus as their ultimate King. The result? The movement of Christianity is the continuing unfolding story of God and humanity. In Matthew 28:19-20 Jesus instructs his followers to unite (in what would later be called the church) around the common purpose of reconciling humans with God—disciplemaking. Jesus' invitation and command

include all peoples, all tribes, all cultures, all classes, all
education levels, the powerful, the weak, those from the
majority culture, the oppressed, and the marginalized. Jesus
began a movement that changed lives and cultures.

Ecclesia-Motus

To see how Jesus' movement changes lives and culture,
we need to combine social movement theory with the
movement markers of the church. The evidence-based
Ecclesia-motus framework[5] was built on the missio-
ecclesiology theoretical framework[4] applying social
movement theory to the Christian church. Ecclesia-
motus describes the church (ecclesia) on a mission or as
a movement (motus). The Ecclesia-motus framework
incorporates the three key DNA dimensions of the church[3]
and the movement markers Jesus wove into the church's
foundation in Matthew chapter 16:13-20.

The Ecclesia-motus framework combines elements of
sociology with theology (socio-theology) to provide a tool
that offers a new perspective for understanding, leading,
and participating in the local church. Ecclesia-motus
describes the church as both gathered and sent, noting
significant relationships between connection with God,
missionally encouraging community, and engagement in
missional living.

The first movement marker in the Ecclesia Motus
framework is a connection with God and His mission.
From our connection with God, we understand our
identity as members of God's family and church. We also
understand our unique identity as someone in Christ, saved
through Jesus, adopted as sons and daughters of God,

and engaging in our role in God's redemptive story. The
second movement marker is participating in a mobilizing
community marked by missional encouragement. As
Christians and part of the Church, we are encouraged and
held accountable to live sent in culture as one serving King
Jesus in every aspect of life: worship, work, family, finance,
government, art, and recreation. The third movement
marker is living sent with God and others in God's mission.
Because the Ecclesia-motus framework applies aspects
of social movement theory to the church, it is important
to connect the dots between the movement markers and
aspects of social movement theory.

Social movement theory has three core elements:
rhetorical, strategic, and cultural[4]. The rhetorical element
in social movement theory informs the large gatherings
of a movement, the authority for the movements, and
the movement's identity, which encourages individuals
to adopt the group identity of the movement. One
example of the rhetorical stage might be large meetings
that remind people of the vision and mission of the
movement, challenge them to increase their participation,
and encourage them to increase their identification with
the movement and its goals. The rhetorical element in
the Ecclesia-motus framework focuses on connecting
with God and His mission. Generally, church worship
gatherings focus on connecting with God through teaching,
sacraments, and worship[15]. However, most scholarship does
not include mission as an essential aspect of a local church.
Yet, in Matthew 16, the movement marker of engaging in
God's mission and the Ecclesia-motus framework suggest

that God's mission is essential to every gathering of Jesus' followers.

The strategic element of a social movement is the glue that keeps people engaged in a movement, supported, directed, and willing to engage in collective action. While the rhetorical element answers the question of 'who?' or 'why me?', the strategic element answers the question of 'why here and why now?'. Smaller gatherings of local cells or chapters in a movement may be exemplars of the strategic phase. Because the rhetorical authority and mission of the movement inform identity and purpose, movement leadership becomes stronger through decentralization. The strategic element in the Ecclesia-motus framework focuses on community and missional encouragement. Identity and purpose are reinforced and normalized in smaller communities marked by missional encouragement. Missional encouragement helps people answer the questions of "Why me, why here, why now?" and helps people make plans to act personally or as part of a group. The effectiveness of decentralized leadership in social movements raises the question: How do the traditional hierarchical leadership models of the Western church impede the movement nature of the church?

The final element of social movement theory, which pertains to the movement of the church, is the cultural element. The cultural engagement element focuses on how those involved in a movement will protest through action to achieve the movement's mission. Following identity formation and strategic planning, collective action emerges in a movement, engaging in constructive change. Various mechanisms such as protests, boycotts, lobbying, legislation, sharing stories, or art are examples of the cultural element of social movements. The cultural element of the Ecclesia-motus framework focuses on missional living or living sent. Understanding the various mechanisms for expressing God's redemptive mission through Jesus Christ to an antagonistic culture is the essential work of the strategic phase. But good planning without any action produces nothing. Historically, the Christian Church has been committed to the flourishing of people, communities, and the surrounding culture. Christianity's prosocial behavior has contributed constructively to society, including art and architecture, hospitals and orphanages, and education and fair labor standards[8]. The Christian church was instrumental in social justice and civic engagement for the marginalized, in the sanctity of life, abortion, infanticide, freedom from slavery, and the equality of women. The movement marker embracing God's gospel mission and the church's mission is essential. Therefore, the missional mobilization described through the Ecclesia-motus framework must foster accountability that leads to action. The world needs the church to engage in culture because people flourish under the compassion, care, and leadership of those who follow Jesus.

Knowing the Marks

As early as the mid-1990s, scholars sounded the alarm that the Christian church was losing attendees and influence in Western Europe[16]. Despite the warnings of scholars and theologians and the resurgence of some churches, the Western church continues to struggle in Europe[17]. Over

two decades and a global pandemic later, the alarm bells
are going off for the Western church of the Global North
in the United States. The church must revive or continue
the trajectory of Western Europe, which is losing ground in
attendance and cultural influence. Churches in the United
States cannot remain divided over non-essential concerns,
nationalism, and being known for what Christians are
against while ignoring the priority of God's mission.
The Western Church in the United States must change
its trajectory, finding new life and hope in Jesus' divine
authority, the community of His body, and living sent,
empowered by the Holy Spirit on God's mission with Jesus.

Ecclesia-motus provides a new perspective and
a balanced approach to engaging in the movement of
the Christian church. Ecclesia-motus is an evidence-
based framework that outlines the church's structure as a
movement and describes how the movement markers work
together. Connecting with God and His mission as a large
group, a gathering, a church—brings purpose and direction
to our small groups or smaller communities and how we
live on mission as a part of the church daily. The smaller
church communities provide missional encouragement and
accountability, reinforcing our connection with God and His
mission and helping us engage in missional living. As we
live sent with God, we increase our connection with God
and His mission. Divine knowledge or connecting with God
and His mission is good, but we miss the movement if we
are never challenged or mobilized toward God's mission.
Ecclesia-motus provides a new perspective, challenging
how we view the Church and how we lead and engage in
the local church and our daily lives.

The problem of diminishing attendance and influence facing the Western Church in the United States did not happen overnight. Concerns about the Church in the United States following the same trajectory as the Church in Western Europe increased following the COVID-19 pandemic. Approximately ten million people did not return to church physically or virtually[18], and for many, church attendance became optional[19]. However, there is hope. We will not find an instant fix; long-term problems require long-term solutions. While defining moments in a generation like the COVID-19 pandemic may illuminate or exacerbate problems, other moments, such as September 11, 2001, may cause people to seek God in large numbers. We must engage in the long-term revitalization effort of the Western church, ready for God to move. We need to be ready for the next defining moment, the next move of the Spirit, the next revival. The church must revive. Therefore, how we lead must change, how we engage in the church must change, and how we live our lives must change. The church must revive, and if you are reading this, you need to answer three questions before going any further: Why you? Why here (where you live, work, and play)? And why now? God is on the move; will you join Him?

CHAPTER 3 – END NOTES

1. Stark, R. (1997). *The Rise of Christianity: How the Obscure, Marginal Jesus Movement Became the Dominant Religious Force in the Western World in a Few Centuries.* HarperSanFrancisco.

2. NIH. (2024, December 9). *Deoxyribonucleic Acid (DNA).* National Human Genome Research Institute. https://www.genome.gov/genetics-glossary/Deoxyribonucleic-Acid-DNA

3. Cole, N. (2005). *Organic church: Growing faith where life happens* (1st edition). Jossey-Bass.

4. Leffel, G. P. (2007). *Faith seeking action: Mission, social movements, and the Church in motion.* Scarecrow Press.

5. Strecker, J. (2020). *Church effectiveness: Organizational culture, religioisty, sense of community and civic engagement* [Dissertation].

6. Stark, R. (2006). *Cities of God: The real story of how Christianity became an urban movement and conquered Rome.* HarperOne.

7. Nystrom, D. (2013). We have no king but Caesar. In S. McKnight & J. B. Modica (Eds.), *Jesus Is lord, Caesar is not: Evaluating empire in New Testament studies* (pp. 23–37). InterVarsity Press.

8. Schmidt, A. J. (2009). *How Christianity changed the world.* Zondervan.

9. Keller, T. (2020, September 18). *Justice in the Bible*. Life in the Gospel. https://quarterly.gospelinlife.com/justice-in-the-bible/

10. Heiser, M. (2015). *The Unseen Realm: Recovering the Supernatural Worldview of the Bible*. Lexham Press.

11. Wright, N. T. (2016). *How god became king: The forgotten story of the gospels* (Reprint edition). HarperOne.

12. Conerly, T. R., Holmes, K., & Tamang, A. L. (2022). *Introduction to sociology 3e*. Independently published.

13. Addison, S., & Stetzer, E. (2012). *What Jesus started: Joining the movement, changing the world* (Illustrated edition). IVP Books.

14. Addison, S. (2021). Why movements rise and fall. In W. Farah (Ed.), *Motus Dei: The Movement of God to Disciple the Nations*. William Carey Library.

15. Grudem, W. A. (2020). *Systematic theology: An introduction to biblical doctrine* (2nd ed.). Zondervan Academic.

16. Davie, G. (1994). *Religion in Britain since 1945*. Blackwell Publishers.

17. Bartholomä, P. (2024). Growth against the trend? - Reflections on the current state of mission among Free Churches in Germany. In R. Kunz & H. Wrogemann (Eds.), *Mission in Crisis: The Unfinished Homework of the Church*. Evangelische Verlagsanstalt.

18. Rotolo, M., & Nortey, J. (2023, March 28). How the Pandemic Has Affected Attendance at U.S. Religious Services. *Pew Research Center*.

https://www.pewresearch.org/religion/2023/03/28/how-the-pandemic-has-affected-attendance-at-u-s-religious-services/

19. Earls, A. (2023, June 15). *Reversing the Shrinking Share of Americans Who Regularly Attend Church*. Lifeway Research. https://research.lifeway.com/2023/06/15/reversing-the-shrinking-share-of-americans-who-regularly-attend-church/

CHAPTER 4

BRIDGES TO THE FUTURE

Brothers and sisters, I do not consider myself to
have taken hold of it. But one thing I do: Forgetting
what is behind and reaching forward to what is
ahead, I pursue as my goal the prize promised by
God's heavenly call in Christ Jesus.
Philippians 3:13-14

God's church will always have a future. It is God's
mission, not the church's mission, and God's
mission will be carried out with or without our
tribes and traditions.
Leonard Sweet, *Rings of Fire*

Building Bridges

Long before the popularity of the ground lava game, my
brother and I would play a game lofted in the Vine Maples
of the Pacific Northwest. Adjacent to our trailer's campsite
grew a twisting grove of Vine Maples. The trees were three
to five inches in diameter and had grown up forming
intertwined forest highways over the stumps of centuries-
old trees. Our game wasn't about the ground being lava,
but a game of tag in which being tagged or falling out of a

tree and touching the ground made you it. The goal was to
jump from tree to tree and chart a course across the would-
be forest as we ran through the grove. Two kids running
through the woods playing a part tag and part follow-
the-leader game resonates with the essential leadership
responsibility of building the bridge as you walk across it[1].

Our path, or bridge, was unknowable as we ran
through the trees until we were right on top of it. Racing
through the Vine Maples, we built our bridge as we ran
and followed each other. The empty churches and sparse
congregations littering the European continent[2] tell of
potential storms in the near distance for churches in the
United States. The storm sirens alert: the church must
revive. Today, the Western church faces losing momentum,
people, and influence. Yet, since every church is different,
it is irresponsible to prescribe a one-size-fits-all solution.
Because every church is different, there is no one bridge
leading to beneficial change, no secret sauce, no try these
shifts, and no do these three application points, and your
church and community will flourish. As we explore how to
lead and engage the local church as a movement, we will
need a plan to build the bridge as we lead others across
it, adapting to the twists and turns of our church's unique
missional path.

I have grown a lot between the carefree days
of running barefoot on trees during Washington state
summers and the declaration that the church must revive.
My growth has led me to realize the significance of our
responsibility as church leaders, from the innocent joy
of childhood to the serious task of guiding the church
through necessary changes. We need to reimagine and

reembrace the forms and functions of the local church; we need to reinvent the way we lead and reinvite those we lead into the urgent mission of Jesus. We will also need a new framework to help shift our thinking about the church from what we have known to where we are going. As leaders, it is our job to understand history, to exegete the present times, and to plot a course toward the future. Yet even though we are discerning, strategic, and informed by those who have gone before us, as leaders, we are always building bridges as we walk across.

Bridges of the Past

Do you remember the Mustangs from the 1980s? The car, not the horse. I like many newer Mustang models, but I am a fan of the classics—the 60's and 70's Mustangs. Just not the 80's Mustangs. Don't get me wrong, the 1980s Mustangs still drove and handled like a sports car and were definitely fun to drive. The 1980s Mustangs also had a strong engine, a more efficient fuel economy, and technological improvements that made the Mustang safer and better for the environment. The 1980s Mustangs were better for the planet even though they lacked some of the allure of their earlier models. The truth is, like it or not, despite their less-than-appealing exterior, the 1980s Mustangs were necessary for the new electric Mustangs on the market today. We learn from the past as we build bridges forward. The bridges of the past held firm in their time. We need to learn from past leaders, past ministry models, strategies, and methods of the church. Our learning helps us see the path forward and build bridges that will be as effective today as the bridges of the past were in their time.

We may need to take a few steps backward to get unstuck occasionally, but going backward rarely helps you build bridges effectively for the future. Let's go back to the 1965 Mustang. Wait, it is nearly impossible to find regular gasoline, let alone enough gasoline to power a 289 4-barrel Shelby engine running about eleven miles to the gallon. Likewise, it doesn't make sense, or is it practical, to say, "To help our church, let's go back to the first-century church." We learn from history and change and grow because of the past, not to become the past.

Face it, many of the problems with people leaving the Western church are the result of the activities of the Western church. Youth ministries hyped up the youth church experience with great music, powerful worship, fun games, and targeted teaching and opportunities. When those students graduated high school, many found that the church of adults was nothing like the church they knew. In 2007, Willow Creek Community Church evaluated and reported on its practices in the book *Reveal: Where Are You?* At the time, Willow Creek hosted thousands of weekly attendees at multiple campuses with a passion for reaching those far from following Jesus. The report revealed that Willow Creek's leadership strategically involved people far from Christ in various church activities to help them surrender to Jesus and learn to follow Him[3]. However, their study also revealed that the same strategy used to reach people was limiting the growth of most of their Christian attendees.

There was a time in recent history when mass evangelism events would fill stadiums, and hundreds, if not thousands, would surrender to Jesus in person and through the event's televised broadcast. Parachurch ministries had access to build relationships and share the good news of Jesus with students on public school campuses, colleges, and universities. Youth events offering free pizza might attract hundreds of students. The community and the culture recognized the church as a safe place, and the general population respected ministers and ministries. During this cultural moment, the strategies and methods produced momentum for gospel-advancing ministry, respect for the church and clergy, and a season of cultural favor. The world is different now; the culture no longer favors Christianity. It doesn't mean that the bridges of the past were wrong or bad. God used the past efforts of churches and church leaders to significantly impact their congregations, communities, and surrounding cultures— the right tools at the right time. As we face new challenges, declining church involvement, diminished respect of church leaders, and five or more generations actively represented in our local churches, we need the right tools for today. Yes, we must learn from the past. But today, we must use different materials and tools to lead the church and build the bridge we are currently walking on.

First, We Need to Get Unstuck

The church must revive, but before we begin building a bridge to help the church change and exploring a framework for strengthening the bridge, we need to be on the same page and in the same category. Each of us brings our personal history with us each day. We also bring our church history, filled with joys, successes, failures, and hurts, into our daily leadership. Any book that offers an all-encompassing approach to changing the church and promises to work everywhere and for everyone would be overselling itself. This book aims to provide a framework, basic building materials, and a direction or vision for helping every church become more effective in our changing and turbulent cultures.

For many years, the Western church has been a place for people to gather, a refuge for those who are hurting, and hope for those willing to enter its doors and find shelter. While viewing the church as a destination will, and to some extent should, continue, we need other ways of thinking about the church. The purpose of this book is not to address the church as a destination but to present a picture of the church as a launching or sending agent for Jesus' kingdom purposes. If a pendulum is swinging between the church as a gathering and the church as a sending agency, we have swung too far toward the gathering. Therefore, this book proposes to focus less on methods for making local churches great again and more on mobilizing every individual for their role in Jesus' kingdom purpose.

You may have made a category mistake if you read this book to discover methods or programs to change your church. We find a simple example of a category mistake in the science and Biblical revelation debate. Often, those arguing against the Bible and defending the findings of science note that the Bible is not always scientifically accurate. As Christians who believe the Bible is the Word of God, it can be difficult not to be drawn into an argument defending the Bible. But this argument is based on a category mistake. Science is about recording what humans have observed. If we observe the same

REVIVE   92

phenomenon enough times, our certainty grows, and we declare our feeling of certainty as scientific fact. Scientific proofs do not make things true. When things are true, science can discover proof. The Bible is not about recording human observations of God. Instead, God reveals Himself, His work, and His ways to humanity. Observation and revelation are two separate categories. We spent so much time in the latter half of the 20th century concerned with where people were going when they died that we ignored the target audience of the great commission—those who are following Jesus. Even if you read this book wanting to make your church a larger destination, I hope you are becoming convinced that the church's mission is making disciplemakers—to mobilize people in the movement of Jesus' kingdom. To accomplish our mission, the church must revive, not simply try to do better.

Accepting Our History

Our problem is with our histories, past experiences, preferences, and even how our families engaged or didn't engage with church. Because of our histories, we struggle to get past pictures and concepts of our church experiences out of our heads. Neil Cole, in his book *Church 3.0: Upgrades For The Future of The Church,* introduces fifteen shifts[5], with some repetition, that he believes are essential for the flourishing of the Western church. Cole's suggested shifts toggle between methods (gathering) and mobilization (going). These shifts focus on three categories: the church's environment, leadership, and the church's engagement in the community.

The environment shifts include moving from rows to circles, anonymity to intimate relationships, and modeling church life after that of a family rather than an academic institution. Most of the environmental shifts focus on the church gathered, and are dependent on the size and location (rural/urban), and tradition of the a church. The leadership shifts Cole sees necessary for the church's future include shifting from institutional leadership development to fieldwork development, ordained pastors to ordinary ministry practitioners, and from singular lead pastors to gifted team leadership. Cole's leadership shifts suggest a plurality of leadership. The shifts affecting the church's community engagement include shifting from growing by addition to multiplication, from a focus on attractional ministry to mobilizing the church, from bringing in outside resources to employing indigenous resources, from classroom education to cohorts, from high operating budgets to low operating budgets, from conducting most ministry at church campuses to ministering in the community.

Finally, Cole suggests the church needs new measures of success, shifting from success based on seating capacity to embracing success based on sending activity. Many of Cole's shifts envision potential bridges for the future. However, some carry the weighty echoes of past effectiveness and paradigms of the church. Yet, all of Cole's shifts cry out that the church must revive.

Don't worry; this book's proposed changes do not address the Church's foundational beliefs, sacraments, and ordinances. Most Christian traditions accept that Christian churches or congregations' foundational structures, forms, and practices involve gathering Christians for fellowship, teaching, and worship—including participation in the ordinances[6]. This book's aim is not about the church gathered but rather to re-vision what the church might look like as a launching or sending agent for Jesus' kingdom purposes. This book also seeks to help us shed leadership preconceptions and transition away from internal organizational metrics, focusing on health and vitality, to external metrics, focusing on kingdom mission and community engagement.

Moving Forward Has a Cost

The church must revive. But real and beneficial change takes time, resilience, and time. No, I didn't mess that up; I said time twice. Real change takes a lot of time, and if you get the opportunity to be there--the process will demand resilience. Simply put, change is never easy.

We all want the easy button or the secret sauce to expand Jesus' kingdom or make our churches grow. Historically, periods of widespread revivalism, evangelistic campaigns, and rapid or expansive church growth resulted in the rise of a select group of prominent pastors and leaders. These figures, championed by many as heroes of the faith, have gained influence through the stories of their ministries' dramatic expansion. It makes sense to celebrate with those who succeed. However, we need to be cautious for two reasons. First, the higher the pedestal, the greater the fall. Too often, Christian leaders who have genuinely added to the work of the kingdom have had moral failures, hurting the people closest to them and marring their legacies. The second caution focuses less on the star leader and more on us. Too often, we want the same growth, the same reviving of our people and communities, and sometimes the accolades accompanying success. We conclude that if we did what they did, we would get what they got. But change, real change, doesn't come easily, and it rarely comes fast. We can see the Church and our churches change through consistency, patience, and resilience.

The problem with time is that time usually outlives us. Time may outlive our tenure at a church, our willingness to serve, or our mortal bodies. The resilient leader must, therefore, choose between leading for results that they will personally experience or leading for results that may not blossom during their time.

Antonio Gaudi was a twenty-nine-year-old architect in Barcelona, Spain. Young Antonio's desire to call people to follow Jesus drove his initial vision for building a church in Barcelona. Gaudi was the chosen architect of the Sagrada Familia. Gaudi's approach to designing the church emanated from his worship and wonder of God and his desire to declare the good news of Jesus through his art— architecture. Gaudi began work on the Sagrada Familia in 1883 and continued until he died in 1926. Gaudi did not see the completion of his work. The work on the Sagrada Familia has been carried on following Gaudi's original vision and continues to this day as the longest-running construction project in the world. Gaudi was willing to invest himself in results that he wouldn't see to impact people he would never meet.

Gaudi's architecture intersected with his kingdom's calling and purpose, and when a tragic accident cut his life short, his legacy continued. The church must revive. Are you willing to count the cost and commit to building a bridge for the future of the Church? In his famous 1963 address, Dr. Martin Luther King declared his willingness to count the cost of change. "So even though we face the difficulties of today and tomorrow, I still have a dream. It is a dream deeply rooted in the American dream. I have a dream that one day this nation will rise up and live out the true meaning of its creed: We hold these truths to be self-evident, that all men are created equal"[8]. We haven't seen the fruition of Dr. King's dream, but, like Gaudi, his bridge has outlived him. The bridge Dr. King started building as he walked across has borne the weight of many, and as others have continued to build onto his bridge, it is a bridge that continues to bear the weight of the oppressed, outcast, and overlooked.

Great Expectations

The church must revive, but before building the bridge, we must be ready to invest our time because real change takes time. We also know that we must set and stick to our course. We need to be resilient and willing to wait for results. We also need one more thing before we take the first step off the edge and begin walking where there is no bridge. Robert Quinn describes the leader's responsibility to embrace the expectation of vision, "When we commit to a vision to do something that has never been done before, there is no way to know how to get there. We simply have to build the bridge as we walk on it"[1]. We need expectation.

To have expectation, we need to know what to expect. To learn what we need to expect, we must turn to an old leadership saying, "You can only expect what you inspect." As kids, most of us learned that if you put a coin into a gumball machine, you can expect to get a gumball. The coin would drop into the slot; reaching up, you turn the small metal nob clockwise. Once and then, in the second or third rotation, you hear the release of the gumball falling into the dispenser. When we walk on old bridges, what has worked in the past informs our expectations. When building new bridges as we walk on them, what we measure informs our expectations.

In earlier chapters, we discussed how viewing the church as a movement may help us develop additional measures or metrics based on successful social movements or what I call movement success. Movement success combines traditional metrics with mobilizing people toward collective action on mission with God. Traditional metrics measure success by counting how many people attend, give money, and serve regularly. Leading with traditional metrics means inspecting your assets: bodies, buildings, budgets, and baptisms. Traditional measures make sense when assessing the church gathered for weekly worship services, leading teams or committees, and activities. Activities, events, or programs are successful if they improve the church's metrics. In this paradigm, attendance growth and budget stability drive the functions of the church. Traditional metrics will remain useful for managing and maintaining the church gathered or the church as an organization. However, we will not be building new bridges into the church's future unless we add measures of movement success to the traditional church measures.

Effectively leading and mobilizing the church in our current cultural trends demands more than adhering to the conventional metrics of success that have traditionally shaped and guided Western approaches to church leadership and involvement. In our world of scrolling video shorts, you probably already know the answer to the following question. Would you rather have $10,000 a day for thirty days or a penny doubled every day for thirty days? Go ahead, pull out your phone, and do the math. We can trust that multiplication will always be more powerful than addition.

However, addition will always be easier than multiplication. An optimistic church leader spoke to me about opportunities for their congregation to engage their local community. The church leader reported that a church in another community invested heavily in their local schools. He believed his church should do something similar. The church leader had expectations, but the expectations followed a common pattern. A church leader has an idea, casts the vision, develops a strategy or program, galvanizes the vision into a possibility, and mobilizes the others in the church to fulfill his vision. During the startup process, the leader is the champion of the initiative. We can take the scenario to the next level by having the leader pass their role as champion to a new champion. Unfortunately, the ministry initiative only survives if it has a champion who owns the vision. Ministry envisioned and championed by paid church staff is addition, not multiplication. Ministry efforts that rely on addition are using an old bridge. Therefore, even when

transitioning a ministry to volunteer leadership, we often
don't find multiplication; at best, we find complex addition.

We all want the penny doubled each day for
thirty days; we all know multiplication makes more
sense. The problem is that multiplication is similar to
real change; it takes time and requires resilience. Even
though multiplication is challenging, it feels right because
multiplication is organic growth. Last spring, I planted
four tomato plants: three Roma tomato plants and one
Early Girl. I did not plant Cherry tomatoes. I did this
purposefully, wanting to keep my garden simple—two
kinds of tomatoes. The addition is fairly simple: three plus
one equals four. So, why do I have six tomato plants, four
varieties, and one of the plants is a cherry tomato bursting
with little tomatoes everywhere? Simple, sometime last
spring, an unseen, unplanned, outside force of nature
(probably a robin) infused my garden with cherry tomato
seeds. Organic growth within the Church of the living God
feels right because we know that the Holy Spirit, often
unseen and unplanned, infuses His presence and power
into His church. That is why organic growth eats the logic
and scope of organizational strategy for breakfast. To build
a bridge as we walk on it, we need expectation. Expectation
to go where God is calling us, and that God will show up
as He invites His people to join Him on His mission. We
need to set our expectation toward the penny doubled, our
gardens bursting, and people in unplanned-for numbers
surrendering their lives to Jesus. We need to expect the
kingdom; it's organic multiplication. It's movement.

Knowing Isn't Doing

Over the two thousand-plus years of church history, churches have danced back and forth between understanding the church, operating, and measuring effectiveness as a movement and an institution. Pastor Timothy Keller attempted to describe the dance or tension between the church's institutional and movement natures as opposite ends of a competing dynamic[9]. Many people have written about the competing dynamics of the church as a movement, including Timothy Keller[9], Ed Stetzer[10], Steve Addision[11], and Daniel Guder[12]. There is an observed story or life cycle13 in the tension between movement and organization. The life cycle of churches begins as informal movements and, through success and growth, adopt institutional structures and measures for growing organizational or institutional churches. The church dance between institution and movement seems normal, but the dance is more descriptive than prescriptive.

Historically, we see the description of the church in Acts 18-21. During the time Paul is in Ephesus, a guy named Epaphras makes a journey of over 100 miles from Colossae to Ephesus. It is possible that driven by rumors of Paul's message and preaching, Epaphras made the journey only to hear Paul speak, or perhaps Epaphras was in Ephesus doing business when he heard Paul. Either way, while in Ephesus, Epaphras hears the good news and surrenders his life to Jesus. Filled with new life, Epaphras brings the message of God's grace and mercy through Jesus Christ home to Colossae. As Epaphras shared the message, it wasn't long before there was a small collection of Jesus' followers. As the group began to grow, an informal movement was born. The church in Colossae was growing. We learn in the first two verses of the book of Philemon that the growing Colossian church met in Philemon's house.

Over the next 300 years, Christians met in homes. As homes filled, the church spread to new homes, planting new churches. In the beginning of Paul's letter to the Philippian churches, we read that Paul addressed his letter to all the Christians in Philippi (multiple house churches) and the appointed leaders. Here, we see a picture of the early church ecclesial structure. Paul introduces us to overseers and deacons tasked with responsibility for the many churches in Philippi. The responsibilities of the overseers and deacons included spiritual direction, prayer, teaching, care, and protection from false teachers. "Be on guard for yourselves and for all the flock of which the Holy Spirit has appointed you as overseers, to shepherd the church of God, which he purchased with his own blood" (Acts 20:28, CSB). About 300 years into the Church's history, Constantine determined that Christianity would be the empire's religion, formalizing the church as an institution. The responsibility of the overseers and deacons had grown into formal roles and positions, and the many house churches began meeting in large halls and building buildings.

The life cycle of growing churches produces new churches out of the movement, but as a church grows in age and size, the movement gives way to institution[13]. We know that healthy churches should produce new churches and new movements[14]. Historians have noted that the instructional structures do not drive the movement multiplication of churches[13]. One can know much about your church's mission, methods, and even how to accomplish its mission but never move to action. Others argue that well-informed and well-trained congregations will exhibit alignment or a greater unity toward the mission of the church[15]. While alignment is powerful and necessary, alignment does not necessarily propagate movement. The curse of being educated is that you know what to do, even when you don't do it. Some authors and scholars suggest that the Western church is educated beyond their level of obedience. It doesn't matter if you have learned the nine, ten, or twelve indicators of church health. The book of James in the Bible sums up the disparity between knowledge and activity. Knowing isn't doing.

Solutions that involve teaching rarely solve problems that involve doing. As a result, movement multiplication in churches often occurs at the edges of institutional structures[13]. When people seek movement through missional living separate from their current church, a new church may be planted. As the newly planted church is established, leadership activity is divided between focusing on missional activity and maintaining the young church. Leadership develops institutional structures that help serve, organize, and retain people to balance the divided focus. With continued time and growth, leadership activity must focus on the organizational structures of the church. Those engaging in missional activity, once comprising the church's core, are now on the fringe, the edge. Tension grows between maintaining structures and those on the missional edge. Throughout history, people on the edge of the institutional church, responding to the call of missional engagement, have launched missionaries, missionary bands, parachurch ministers and organizations, and church planting. Healthy movement oriented churches, churches with movement DNA, are the best multipliers of disciplemaking movement. are the Unfortunately, movement multiplication often launches out of the institutional church's edges rather than the church's very DNA. How we multiply churches must change. The church must lean less on institutional structures and learn to lean into movement.

Framing the Structure

Yes, the church must revive, but it would be foolish to suggest that it should only lean into movement and have no structure. When organizing groups of people, there is structure. Moses learned that structure is necessary and good. "You will certainly wear out both yourself and these people who are with you, because the task is too heavy for you. You can't do it alone" (Exodus 18:18, CSB). Moses' father-in-law, Jethro, called out a significant leadership problem for Moses. Group leadership is not a single-player game. A plurality of leadership is a strong biblical theme from Genesis through Revelation. Jethro called out a problem but also offered a new leadership framework. Jethro suggested a framework steeped in shared responsibility, ensuring everyone receives care and every voice is heard. Throughout this book, we have covered why the church must revive and how the church must change. And like Jethro, the call to change should be accompanied by a framework providing a pathway or structure toward a solution. Building a bridge while we walk on it doesn't mean that we don't have a plan!

The Ecclesia-motus framework describes the church on mission by combining historical, theological, and practical elements of the church (ecclesia) envisioned as movement (motus) with movement DNA[16]. For church leaders, the Ecclesia-motus framework provides a structure for leading the church as a movement. For all followers of Jesus, the Ecclesia-motus framework provides a catalyst for everyday engagement in the movement of the church. As a framework, Ecclesia-motus does not dictate a church's form, size, or organizational structure. Ecclesia-motus gives us a picture frame through which we see the church as a movement, we can lead the church as a movement, and we can participate in the movement of the church. Ecclesia-motus introduces the need for movement leadership and every follower of Jesus to participate in the movement of the church.

The Ecclesia-motus framework embodies three key dimensions of movement leadership derived from research on social movements: a connection with God and His mission, missional encouragement, and living sent together. At first glance, the Ecclesia-motus framework appears simple and may seem like common sense. The rhythms of connecting with God, connecting with others, and living on mission have been foundational to the Christian church throughout the centuries. We first see the rhythms found in the Ecclesia-motus framework in Genesis 2:15, "The Lord God took the man and placed him in the garden of Eden to work it and watch over it" (Genesis 2:15, CSB). First, we have a connection with God; man was with God in God's garden temple--Eden. We also know from the Genesis account that God determined that man should not be alone;

he needed to connect with others. And finally, the humans had a purpose—to work and watch over the garden. From the beginning of God's great story, we find that humans are hardwired to connect with God, connect with others, and engage in meaningful mission or purpose.

New Measures

The Ecclesia-motus framework is an evidenced-based model[16], providing a new lens for leading churches, engaging in the church's movement, and measuring a church's success or effectiveness. Past measures of church success focused on the person and position of the leaders and on the church as an institution. We will discuss the

Connect with God
and Mission
(large groups)

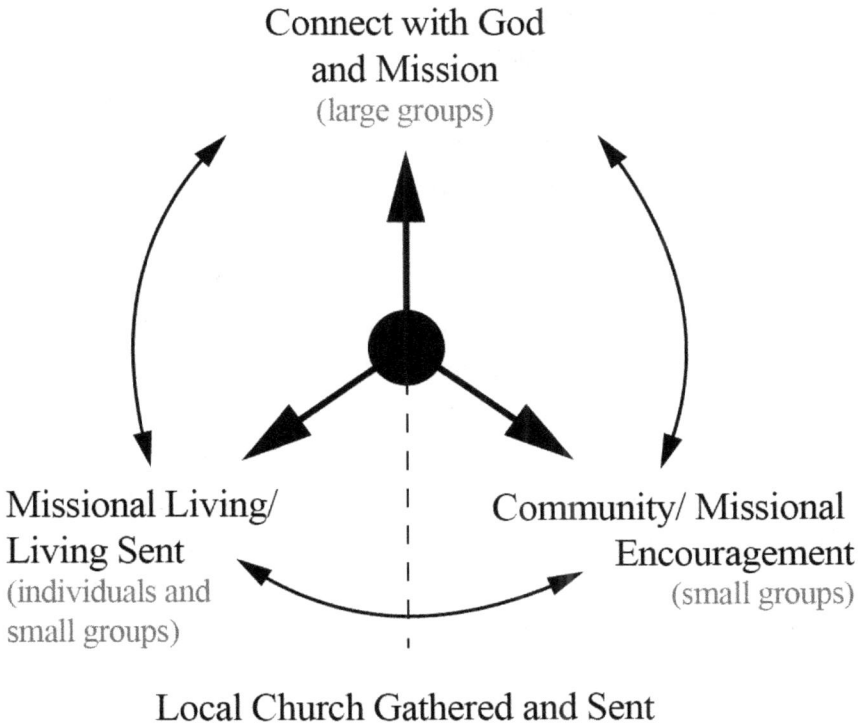

Missional Living/
Living Sent
(individuals and
small groups)

Community/ Missional
Encouragement
(small groups)

Local Church Gathered and Sent

person and position of leadership more in the next chapter on movement and Shepherding Leadership. Numerous measures of success focusing on the institutional aspects of the church can be overwhelming, inconsistent, and elusive[17], leading scholars and experts to conclude that no common definition of church success exists[18]. Scholars and church leaders have tried various approaches to find the best metrics to help the church flourish, such as using The Balanced Scorecard, a common business measurement tool used to define and measure church success[19]. While turning to the business world makes sense for some church leaders, other church leaders feel the business world cannot speak into the spiritual and movement nature of the church, suggesting the need to measure the church differently[9]. Others have summarized church organizational outcomes as identity formation, belonging within community, and positive engagement of the world and culture. In their research with teenagers and young adults, Kara Powell and Brad Griffin echoed a relational approach, highlighting the importance of identity, belonging, and purpose as central to being human and vital for effective church ministry[20].

Some argue that the church is not a business. Why measure anything in the first place? As we embark on the journey of building the bridge as we walk on it, we need to remember the relationship between expecting and inspecting. We can only expect what we inspect. If God were to ask you: "Why does the church you are serving in or attending exist?" What would you say? Likewise, how would you respond to the question: "Why is your church in its current location?" And finally: "What is unique to Jesus'

kingdom about the variety of people currently attending
your church?"

Dr. Colby Kinser, the EFCA Midwest district
superintendent, reframes these questions as follows: Why
here? Why us? Why now? What you measure leads to what
you do and reveals what you believe about your purpose
as a leader and the purpose of your church. I appreciate Dr.
Kinser's questions because they address the institution and
movement natures of the church. Institutionally, you can
answer why here, us, and now based on the people, place,
and opportunities crafting a global mission for your church.
It is also very likely that traditional measures of church
success may help assess the organizational activity of the
church. However, the church is more than an organization.
So, you can also ask the why here, us, and now questions
for every small group and person in your church. A
church's leadership might craft and agree on the same
organizational mission, but what happens when suddenly
every small group and every individual is launched into
the everyday movement of the church in their community
and world? Three simple questions, asked and answered,
can launch a multiplying movement. Traditional measures
of church success can't keep up with the organic growth
that results from a movement. The church must revive.
Therefore, we must change our definitions and measures
for success.

The Ecclesia-motus framework provides three
key domains for a new set of measures for the church—
connection with God and His mission, connection with
others, and living sent together. The new measures
derived from the Ecclesia-motus framework provide the

raw material we need as we step out on the bridge we are building. First, we must develop our expectations. We need to develop specific expectations for personally connecting with God and His mission and what it looks like for our church to do so. Many Western churches have recognized the need for people to connect as large congregations and in smaller groups each week. What do we expect from these groups? How do we ensure these groups are practicing encouraging missional community? The third dimension is living sent on God's mission. What are our expectations for living with God on His mission each day? What do we expect from the people attending the churches we lead?

As leaders, what do we expect from our times connecting with God? In "Prevailing Prayer," D.L. Moody recounts a powerful story setting our expectations for our time connecting with God and His mission[21]. Moody was challenged by a friend to invest more time in connecting with God through prayer. Reflecting on his habits, Moody began to prioritize longer, more intentional times with God, allowing him to experience greater closeness with God and effectiveness in his ministry. My youth pastor, Chris Renzelman, first shared Moody's story and conclusion with me when I was still in high school. The discipleship group of high school boys led by our Chris was on the verge of ending due to our busy schedules. We took a cue from Moody's life and chose to meet at 5:30 AM each week. Our meetings continued for over two years, launching multiple teenagers into lifelong ministry and engagement in the mission of Jesus' kingdom. Getting teenagers up at 5:30 AM each week might seem impossible. It's just as impossible as building a bridge as you walk on it. Yet, new measures

will provide new paths as we navigate the bridges we are
crossing while leading others in the church.

The first domain of the Ecclesia-motus framework,
connecting with God and His mission, focuses on outcomes,
not activities. Institutions focus on activities; movements
focus on outcomes. I am not saying that activities are absent
as people connect with God. The general assumption is that
as a church, you are meeting for worship, teaching, prayer,
and sacraments as defined by your faith tradition. Your
activity should also involve a plan or pathway for teaching
people to obey all that Jesus commanded (Matthew: 28:20).
From the perspective of leading the church, the focus or aim
is outcomes, not activities. Our expectation is not to target
"that" people are connecting with God and His mission, but
to focus on the results when they "do" connect with God
and His mission. Concerning a weekly worship gathering,
are we asking, "If people connected with God and His
mission today, what results should we be seeing this week,
month, or year?" The transformation of the human heart
by the triune God is God's work. We don't expect our
efforts to transform people, we expect God to transform
people. Therefore, what do we inspect if we expect people
to connect with God and His mission during our weekly
services and ministries? We expect transformed lives.
We inspect transformed lives through stories and values.
Stories of how God is at work and changing the people in
our churches. Stories of how people choose to value what
Jesus values. Are Jesus' kingdom values present in the
people we lead? Do their priorities reflect Jesus' priorities?
God's transforming work will be revealed as we spend time
with people and learn their stories. As we learn the stories

of the people we serve, we listen, respecting the uniqueness of every person for how God is shaping their identity and values.

Once we have identified our expectations and what we will inspect, we must realign our efforts and activities toward our new measures. There is significance in remaining silent concerning the content of the new measures. Determining the importance and weight of different scriptures has birthed many churches and denominations. The church must change, not necessarily in its beliefs, but in how churches are led, how Christ's followers are mobilized on Jesus' kingdom mission, and how the church engages in movement. For this book's context, a church's theological and denominational distinctives are far less important than the church's ability to mobilize attendees on mission with God.

The second domain of the Ecclesia-motus framework is connecting with others in a community of missional encouragement. Many churches have smaller group ministries such as small groups, Sunday morning classes, and Bible studies. Small groups are an effective way to help people connect and remain connected in a church. Smaller groups foster deeper relationships among attendees. Smaller groups can be used to reinforce teaching, facilitate serving opportunities, study the Bible, pray for one another, and peer care and support. Some small groups also include a level of accountability for Christian living. According to the Ecclesia-motus framework, smaller communities should also facilitate missional mobilization. A new type of accountability arises when we target the expectation that our smaller groups encourage missional living. Our

small groups hold one another accountable for engaging
with God on His mission. We can measure, encourage,
and hold one another accountable through sharing our
stories. Stories of how we engage others, how we fail to
focus on God, or how God surprised us with an unforeseen
opportunity to serve others or proclaim Jesus. The content
of the stories will be shaped by how your church defines
and describes God's mission. Yet, as we share our stories
of engaging in God's mission throughout the week, we are
challenged, we are encouraged, and our commitment to
engage in the everyday movement of the church increases.

The third domain of the Ecclesia-motus framework
is living sent on God's mission with Him. How do we
measure the everyday engagement of Jesus' kingdom
mission in the community, at work, at school, shopping,
on a sports team, at a club meeting, or wherever your
day takes you? At first glance, it sounds like herding
cats or trying to wrangle a small group of middle school
boys long enough to get through a brief lesson. Not to
sound repetitive, but we measure living sent primarily
through learning the stories of those we serve and lead.
The measure is in the stories of how individuals and small
groups engage in everyday mission with God. Stories of
lived experience encourage, support, validate, and unite
followers of Jesus engaged in the movement of the church,
living the everyday mission of Jesus' kingdom. Sharing
stories is not a new method for measuring the success
of churches. In my early years of following Jesus, I was
involved with a church that had regular times for sharing
testimonies of God working in and through His people.
A priority on teaching, church size, increased information

to take in, and the busyness of Western culture may have limited the frequency of testimony services. Sharing and hearing such testimonies or stories is a good measure and may help shape your church's identity and culture through the way people describe joining with God in His mission.

Catch the wave

The Ecclesia-motus framework is an evidence-based framework describing the relationships between connecting with God and His mission, connecting with an encouraging missional community, and living sent with God on His mission. While more research is needed on the framework, the evidence directs us to a reality. A relationship exists between the framework's domains, and each domain informs and supports the others. That means—I connect with God and His mission more when I am in a missionally encouraging small group. I connect better in my small group when I am living sent every day with God on mission. As I engage in Jesus's kingdom mission daily, I connect more with God and others. Each domain of the Ecclesia-motus framework supports and builds up the other domains. Take one away, and the others diminish. Invest in all three, and we are building bridges as we run across. As we run on the bridge, together with God and others, as we build it, we know we are part of THE movement.

CHAPTER 4 – END NOTES

1. Quinn, R. E. (2004). *Building the Bridge As You Walk On It: A Guide for Leading Change* (1st edition). Jossey-Bass.

2. Davie, G. (1994). *Religion in Britain since 1945*. Blackwell Publishers.

3. Parkinson, C., & Hawkins, G. (2007). *REVEAL:WHERE ARE YOU?* (First Edition). Willow Creek Association.

4. Packiam, G., & Kinnaman, D. (2022). *The Resilient Pastor: Leading Your Church in a Rapidly Changing World*. Baker Books.

5. Cole, N. (2010). *Church 3.0: Upgrades for the Future of the Church*. John Wiley & Sons.

6. Grudem, W. A. (2020). *Systematic theology: An introduction to biblical doctrine* (2nd ed.). Zondervan Academic.

7. Episode 281: La Sagrada Família. (2019, May 21). *99% Invisible*. https://99percentinvisible.org/episode/la-sagrada-familia-2/

8. King, M. L., Jr. (2023, January 16). Read Martin Luther King Jr.'s "I Have a Dream" speech in its entirety. *NPR*. https://www.npr.org/2010/01/18/122701268/i-have-a-dream-speech-in-its-entirety

9. Keller, T., Chester, T., Montgomery, D., Cosper, M., & Hirsch, A. (2016). *Serving a movement: Doing balanced, gospel-centered ministry in your city*. Zondervan.

10. Addison, S., & Stetzer, E. (2012). *What Jesus started: Joining the movement, changing the world* (Illustrated edition). IVP Books.

11. Addison, S. (2021). Why movements rise and fall. In W. Farah (Ed.), *Motus Dei: The Movement of God to Disciple the Nations*. William Carey Library.

12. Guder, D. L., Barrett, L., Dietterich, I., Hunsberger, G., Roxburgh, A., & Van Gelder, C. (1998). *Missional church: A vision for the sending of the church in North America* (D. L. Guder, Ed.). Wm. B. Eerdmans Publishing.

13. Finke, R., & Stark, R. (2005). *The Churching of America, 1776-2005: Winners and losers in our religious economy* (Revised edition). Rutgers University Press.

14. McLoughlin, W. G. (1978). *Revivals, awakening and reform: An essay on religion and social change in America, 1607-1977*. University of Chicago Press.

15. Snyder, R. (2024). *Messaging the Mission: Developing and Implementing a Messaging Strategy for the Mission Statement of Monticello Christian Church - ProQuest* [Doctoral Dissertaion, Liberty Universtity]. https:// www.proquest.com/openview/5be48ad7a34707ff0abe6c040c65be9d/1? pq-origsite=gscholar&cbl=18750&diss=y

16. Strecker, J. A. (2023). Church Effectiveness: Organizational Culture, Religiosity, Sense of Community, and Civic Engagement [ProQuest Dissertations & Theses]. https://www.proquest.com/docview/3171540225/ FC51726E9A3D46E3PQ/1?sourcetype=Dissertations%20&%20Theses

17. Myers, P. K. (2017). *Authentic leadership and its relationship to ministerial effectiveness among pastors in the church of the Nazarene* [Doctor of Philosophy, Indiana Wesleyan University]. https://www.proquest.com/openview/687bff9c54aafa73c359c8443d4f4fbb/1?pq-origsite=gscholar&cbl=18750&diss=y

18. Webb, R. J. (1974). Organizational Effectiveness and the Voluntary Organization. *Academy of Management Journal, 17*(4), 663–677. https://doi.org/10.5465/255645

19. Boggs, W. B., & Fields, D. L. (2010). Exploring organizational culture and performance of Christian churches. *International Journal of Organization Theory & Behavior, 13*(3), 305–334. https://doi.org/10.1108/IJOTB-13-03-2010-B001

20. Powell, K., & Griffin, B. M. (2021). *3 big questions that change every teenager: Making the most of your conversations and connections.* Baker Books.
Moody, D. L. (1884). *Prevailing Prayer: What Hinders It?* Fleming H. Revell.

CHAPTER 5

SHEPHERDING LEADERSHIP

"Therefore, everyone who hears these words of mine and acts on them will be like a wise man who built his house on the rock. The rain fell, the rivers rose, and the winds blew and pounded that house. Yet it didn't collapse, because its foundation was on the rock. But everyone who hears these words of mine and doesn't act on them will be like a foolish man who built his house on the sand. The rain fell, the rivers rose, the winds blew and pounded that house, and it collapsed. It collapsed with a great crash."
Matthew 7:24-27

"The Secret to success is good leadership, and good leadership is all about making the lives of your team members or workers better."
Tony Dungy

Future Impact

As a youth pastor, I often talked to students about the potential future significance of what now seems like insignificant decisions. Discussions like these with teenagers are rarely simple, so I would often turn to rocket science to illustrate the importance of our choices. I would run two lines of yarn across the room from one side to the other. The taught straight lines indicated no deviation from what is true. I had a student stand with a yardstick at the beginning edge of the lines. Then, I would ask the student to angle the yardstick away from the line to indicate an insignificant bad choice. Students usually picked a point just inches off the yarn. I would then move the far end of one yarn line, aligning it with the student's measurement. The room would grow quiet as I found the new anchor point, not inches but feet away from the original line. I call it rocket science because NASA encountered this problem attempting to land a rover on Mars. Their calculations were slightly off; they still sent the rover to Mars, but they hit Mars, destroying the rover with years of work and investment. Rocket science shows that small decisions can make a significant impact. The church must revive, and our seemingly insignificant choices today may immensely impact our future.

Leadership Change

Much has been written on leading change within organizations and the organizational structures of the church. If the church will revive and operate as a multiplying movement, then how we lead the church needs to change. The Ecclesia-motus framework provides a picture or model for reframing our vision of the church as a multiplying movement. The church's history is littered with movements that pop up, effect change in people, communities, and society, and slowly fade. The author developed the Ecclesia-motus framework introduced in the last chapter through research and by reading scripture through the lens of sociology. Applying the three dimensions of the Ecclesia-motus framework, connection with God and His mission, engaging in a mission-accountable community, and living sent on Jesus' mission, can provide insights to transform current leadership models into movement leadership.

Co-mingled with our church histories is the pattern of adopting business leadership models for leading churches. Businesses, even while striving to care for employees wholistically, adhere to the foundational function of turning a profit. I have a friend whose hobby is roasting coffee. He is a meticulous coffee roaster, producing coffee with amazing aroma and flavor. He enjoys roasting coffee. So why take the enjoyment of the hobby and make it a small business? Because a hobby-turned-business needs to turn a profit. The demands of profit overrule the hobby's enjoyment. Churches and other non-profits are different. They are not driven by the need to make a profit. Instead, they are driven by a mission, a purpose, or a cause. Churches need a different leadership paradigm than for-profit businesses. Therefore, leading the church to revive must look different than the prescriptions of business leadership experts.

Leadership Foundations

If we focus too much on developing an individual as a leader or training leaders for their specific roles, we miss the point of leadership. A biblical basis for leadership begins in Genesis chapter one. The beginning of Genesis chapter one is generally known as the story of the creation of the cosmos. Genesis chapter one is certainly about creation, but we often over-focus on "what" and "when" God is creating, missing the "how" of creation. By "how," I am not referring to the ex-nihilo creation, that God spoke creation into existence out of nothing. "In the beginning, God created the heavens and the earth. Now the earth was formless and empty, darkness covered the surface of the watery depths, and the Spirit of God was hovering over the surface of the waters" (Genesis 1:1-2, CSB). In the beginning, the earth was chaos. The idea of the waters of the deep, or any deep water, representing chaos is common among the spiritual worldviews of ancient Near East literature[1].

There is a growing recognition among scholars that the first creation account in Genesis chapter one describes God bringing order to chaos as He creates[2]. Genesis provides an amazing picture of the ordering nature of God. God is truly a God of order (1 Corinthians 14:33). We see God ordering toward a purpose in creation. Here, we find the heart of real leadership. Real leadership is bringing or conducting people into a united order for a specific purpose.

My son is very musical. I enjoy music and even play a little guitar, but compared to my son, I am not musical. In his musical pursuits, my son enjoys playing the violin. I enjoy listening to my son play the violin. Through his high school music program, my son has the opportunity to play in the school orchestra. At the beginning of each orchestra concert, the musicians file into their seats on stage. As they settle, they organize their music and their instruments. The orchestra is disordered amid the shuffle of musicians, music stands, and sheet music. The chaos dies instantly as the first chair violinist takes the stage. The orchestra is silent; the first chair plays a note, and everyone tunes in unity to the first chair. The chaos from moments earlier melts into unified harmony. Bringing order toward a purpose is the heart of true leadership. Once the first chair is seated, the conductor takes the podium. With a raise of the baton and gesture, the orchestra explodes into ordered yet complex melodies and harmonies as tens of individuals move and play in unison.

Leadership Beginnings

The creation account in Genesis displays God's leadership through the ordering of people or things toward a purpose. But what about human leadership? Genesis 2:15 is often referenced in conversations about vocation and developing the concept of work within a biblical worldview. "The Lord God took the man and placed him in the garden of Eden to work it and watch over it" (Genesis 2:15, CSB). Yet, debate among theologians and scholars exists over the specific meanings of the Hebrew words often translated with agricultural language[3] to till and work[4]. As the debate dust settles, there is agreement among scholars such as Michael Heiser[5], David Shrock, Miles Pelt, Duane Ortlund[6], and

Blaine Eldredge[7] for shedding the agricultural language in exchange for temple language.

In Genesis 1:28, God gives humanity the responsibility to have dominion or to rule and order the created world. The God who brings order out of Chaos in creation confers the responsibility to bring order into the world. We see humanity bring order in creation first in Genesis 2:20 as Adam names the animals. Names in the Old Testament were more than mere labels. By naming the animals, Adam identified the animals' nature and purpose; by giving a name, Adam exercised dominion and brought order[7]. "The man gave names to all the livestock, to the birds of the sky, and to every wild animal; but for the man no helper was found corresponding to him" (Genesis 2:20, CSB). Adam exercised true leadership by naming the animals.

God created humanity adorned with the mantle of leadership, providing instructions for how humans are to lead. Genesis 2:15 uses a hermeneutic that recognizes Eden as a temple and that humanity's role in the garden temple is to serve and guard or protect. Adam and Eve were priests in the garden temple of God. The priestly aspect of the commands to serve and guard/protect echo Moses' use of the same Hebrew words in Numbers 3:7-8, describing the duties of the Tabernacle Priests. When we tie the ruling commands of Genesis 1:28, also commonly known as the cultural mandate, with priestly duties of serving and protecting, we find a collision of purpose and leadership. Real leadership, or the art of leadership, brings order toward a purpose.

Leadership conferences, seminars, books, and classes that target developing leaders often fail to address aspects of real leadership. Approaching leadership through the traditional role of the leader makes sense in Western culture and even more so in the highly individualistic culture of the United States. Real leadership is not about a person occupying a traditional leadership role. Instead, real leadership is less about the traditional leadership role (the leader as a person or position) and primarily about the responsibility to order or empower others to fulfill a shared purpose[8]. Developing an individual's leadership acumen is worthwhile. Yet, if real leadership is concerned with empowering others toward a shared purpose, simply teaching and training people to lead in a traditional leadership role is not enough.

Scholars suggest three categories when considering leadership: elements peripheral to leadership, the content of leadership knowledge, and the philosophy of leadership[9]. The first and most common category for leadership development contains elements peripheral to leadership, including a leader's traits, personality, skills, drives, emotional intelligence, experience, and style. Anything focusing on the traditional role or person of the leader is peripheral to leadership. Elements peripheral to leadership also focus on skills such as leading groups, attaining goals, and management ability. The second leadership category is the content of leadership knowledge. Leadership knowledge covers everything a leader needs to know about an organization, the organizational culture and surrounding culture, and the leader's specific role. Rost's (1993) third category turns to leadership theory, or what it means to lead others, which embodies shared or collective purpose, collaboration, the empowering of the group, and the general process of social influence. Real leadership is ordering or shepherding groups of people engaged in a collective purpose. If the church is going to revive, we need a new way of understanding and engaging in leadership.

Shepherding Leadership

Building on the three categories of real leadership and the Missio-ecclesia framework, Shepherding Leadership is a leadership model addressing the art of leading rather than the person as a leader. Investing in the "who" of leadership will always be beneficial and help leaders grow. However, real leadership does not necessarily flow out of a well-developed leader. Shepherding Leadership recognizes that the art of leading others involves organizing others to fulfill their responsibility for collective purpose, collective action, and the flourishing of others.

Shepherding Leadership has three components: leading with purpose, leading through an empowering and multiplying process, and leading through principles. Leading with purpose connects people to God and His mission. Leading through an empowering and multiplying process connects people in an accountable missional community. Leading through principles helps keep the people we serve engaged on mission with God. The heart of leadership is bringing order for a purpose; Shepherding Leadership describes how leaders order people for God's purpose.

Shepherding Leadership is like servant leadership[10], which, as a leadership theory, prioritizes empowering others, collaboration, and serving rather than commanding. The desired outcomes of servant leadership, apart from organizational benefit, are personal and professional development and a supportive and engaged community. Shepherding Leadership embodies the priorities of servant leadership but differs from servant leadership in that it focuses on employing real leadership rather than merely on the leader's actions. Shepherding Leadership focuses on identifying and elevating the collective purpose of the group and deemphasizing positional leadership through empowering multiplication and guarding others by ensuring protective principles.

Shepherding Leadership relies on the shepherd metaphor. The shepherd is a common metaphor for leadership. In the Old Testament, God is called the shepherd of His people. In the New Testament, Jesus refers to himself as the good shepherd. Kevin Leman and William Pentak[11] introduce a variant of servant leadership entitled The Way of The Shepherd, prioritizing the team's wellbeing. Their leadership model links traditional leadership with the shepherd's tools to care for their flocks, including the voice, staff, rod, and the shepherd's heart. However, Leman and Pentack present a model focusing on the traditional role of a leader rather than the content of real leadership. Their model of the leader as a shepherd assumes the traditional view of leadership, addressing the character, leadership skills, and the tools a leader uses. The traditional view of leadership and leadership development is beneficial but peripheral to leading [ordering toward a purpose] groups of people. Shepherding Leadership benefits from leaders who are well-equipped with

traditional leadership skills. However, for Shepherding
Leadership, the metaphor of the shepherd is less concerned
with the "who" of the shepherd and more concerned with
how the shepherd organizes others toward a purpose.

The Shepherding Leadership Model

As new generations of Jesus' followers move into
leadership within the Western Church in the United States,
the will change. The church must revive. Too many people
claim the name Christian and occupy seats in weekend
worship services who have not surrendered to Jesus or
prioritized their lives to follow Him[12]. As the surrounding
culture of the West continues to diverge from the values of a
biblical worldview, cultural Christianity, and the traditional
leadership models that produced celebrity-status leaders,
large ministry programs and large buildings may also
continue to evaporate. It is time to turn our focus on how
we lead the church as a kingdom movement.

A screwdriver is a tool with a specific use or
purpose—turning a screw. Yet, I have seen screwdrivers
used ineffectively to pry, dig, chip, and hammer. And yes,
sometimes the screwdriver was in my hand. Why? Because
the screwdriver was in reach. When we use a screw and
a screwdriver correctly, physics tells us that the result
is real work. The screwdriver turns the screw, and the
screw goes into the wood. The relationship between the
screwdriver and the screw is like the relationship between
a commanding leader and their followers. The leader
commands their people, and they follow. Common sense
tells us that without a screwdriver, the screws cannot turn
themselves. Likewise, common sense has led us to believe

we need a commanding leader. Without the command of a skilled leader, the people will scatter. Better yet, we need a well-trained, well-skilled, and hopefully charismatic leader to gather the crowds. More people means more opportunity for the gospel...right?

We discussed the true nature of the church through the Ecclesia-motus framework. The church is gathered to connect with God and His mission, to be encouraged and held accountable to engage in and live on God's mission. This results in a movement of Jesus' followers who are mobilized and sent to proclaim Jesus as good news. The traditional role of the leader is the wrong tool to organize a movement. The church already has a singular leader who is more than competent. "And he subjected everything under his feet and appointed him as head over everything for the church, which is his body, the fullness of the one who fills all things in every way" (Ephesians 1:22-23, CSB). The traditional role of the commanding leader must diminish, and a new model for leading the church, in which everyone follows Jesus Christ as the head of the church, must take root.

Shepherding Leadership.

Shepherding Leadership brings together leadership models, strategies, and tools aligned with the social movement aspects of the Missio-ecclesia framework to create a leadership model committed to the flourishing of others. At the heart of Shepherding Leadership is a teaching approach called andragogy. Andragogy is how adults learn. Adults don't learn by being told; rather, adults will learn what they need to know when the need arises[13]. Shepherding

Leadership recognizes that people flourish when called to be and to be better, not when told to do better.

While not specifically engaging in Shepherding Leadership, a factory operating with the goal of employee flourishing echoes the results of Shepherding Leadership[14]. The leadership of the window screen factory employing over 2000 people identified a problem hindering their employees' flourishing—high health care costs. The company's solution was to provide healthcare solutions for their employees. The result? The employees responded with a desire to do better for themselves and the company. Healthcare costs are down, and production is improving. A screen door factory in Alabama is not a social movement. Still, the employees' response—doing better for their health

(Connect with God
and Mission)
Shepherd's Staff - Guide - Purpose

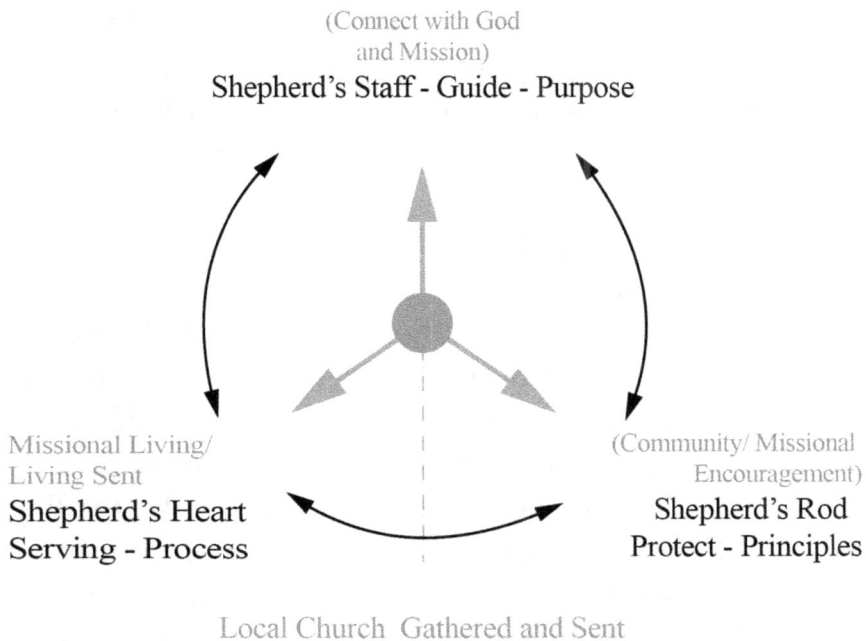

Missional Living/
Living Sent
**Shepherd's Heart
Serving - Process**

(Community/ Missional
Encouragement)
**Shepherd's Rod
Protect - Principles**

Local Church Gathered and Sent

and their employer—isn't something a leader commanded them to do. Leadership committed to the flourishing of others can produce a multiplying effect—a micro-movement within a factory toward increased health and performance.

The Shepherding Leadership model combines the shepherd metaphor, elements of social movement leadership, and the Ecclesia-motus framework to map out how, as church leaders, we can empower and release the church to transform the culture through the good news of Jesus Christ. Shepherding Leadership has three components: leading with purpose, represented by the guidance of the shepherd's staff; leading through an empowering and multiplying process, represented by the shepherd's heart for serving the people and the mission; and leading through principles, represented by the shepherd's rod bringing focus and protection. The Shepherding Leadership model is necessary for the church to be gathered and sent, empowering and releasing the church as a movement.

> Psalm 23 highlights the shepherd metaphor describing how God leads.
> The Lord is my shepherd; I have what I need. He lets me lie down in green pastures; he leads me beside quiet waters. He renews my life; he leads me along the right paths for his name's sake. Even when I go through the darkest valley, I fear no danger, for you are with me; your rod and your staff—they comfort me. You prepare a table before me in the presence of my enemies;

you anoint my head with oil; my cup overflows
(Psalm 23:1-5, CSB).

Shepherding Leadership borrows images from the
shepherd metaphor. The shepherd's staff reflects how God
guides us. The scripture contains many commands to help
humanity follow Jesus, embracing God's purpose and
ways. Yet, Psalm 23 does not describe God's leadership
as demanding or commanding but as inviting, protecting,
empowering, and releasing. God's leadership invites us
to align our hearts and wills with His purposes. God's
leadership protects us, helping us walk the right path and
embrace His calling. God's leadership empowers and
releases us to fully engage in God's purposes.

The Staff – Leading with Purpose

Leading with purpose is grounded in the reality that
Jesus is good news: through Jesus alone, God desires that
everyone might be restored and become fully human.
Through Jesus' life, death, resurrection, and ascension,
every human is invited to participate in our Genesis
1:28 purpose of dominion over creation. Dominion over
creation in Genesis 1:28 refers to responsible stewardship or
management of creation. I like the concept of stewardship
here, as it carries with it the need to act aligned with and
accountable to a higher authority than myself—God. Too
often, we mix up dominion for domination. Dominion
reflects responsibility and authority that is given rather
than taken. Domination, on the other hand, elicits images of
abuses of power, aggressiveness, oppression, exploitation,
and a disregard for the wellbeing of others. Dominion

elicits thoughts of responsibility, while domination elicits thoughts of control. The current cultural conversation about climate change would benefit from a right understanding of dominion versus domination. When domination seeks to take and consume, dominion would call humanity to steward or care for one another and the world we call our home.

Genesis 2:15 refines the human purpose of dominion, imbuing humanity with priestly duties. Understanding the priestly roles of guiding and protecting others is essential to leading purposefully and fulfilling the responsibility of dominion. The shepherd's staff's guidance shows our need to lead with purpose. Leadership emerges when we learn to lead and work out our purpose through the priestly roles of guiding/serving and guarding/protecting. Leading with purpose elevates human purposefulness, culminating in human flourishing. Leading with purpose is not about achieving our goals, ideas, or plans. Leading with purpose is all about serving those we lead through empowering, guiding, reminding, and celebrating their journey toward fulfilling their purpose.

Leading with purpose isn't easy. Leading with purpose focuses on uplifting others, yet it is too easy to want to focus on ourselves. We can forget our purpose even when trying to lead with purpose. Peter Greere's[15] *Mission Drift* explores the common problem of organizations losing sight of their purpose and drifting from their founding mission. *Patrick Lencioni's*[16] *The Five Dysfunctions of a Team* examines how team dynamics can benefit or detract from focusing on the organizational mission. *The Advantage* by Patrick Lencioni[17] reflects on organizational health unified by mission. Alignment around purpose is essential for leadership success. *Good to Great* by Jim Collins[18] looks at the need for companies to maintain their focus on their mission to avoid losing their purpose. *Leading Change* by John P. Kotter[19] deals with maintaining organizational mission while implementing change. Leading change in the church must begin with an unwavering self-sacrificing commitment to purpose.

How do we lead with purpose? First, we must recognize that we connect people to God's mission for the church. Purpose connects to God's mission through a kingdom calling, which describes a local church's unique purpose in its current location and historical time[20]. No matter how large or small your church is, God calls His people to His mission. God invites each person to participate in His mission to fulfill their God-given purpose (Ephesians 2:10). It's not the leader alone who has a purpose that everybody needs to learn and follow. Instead, the Shepherding Leader's job is to help each person in their church embrace God's collective purpose for the Church and their unique calling. As discussed earlier, Jesus designed His church to connect to God and His mission. Airo[21] has developed The Missions Course to help Western churches recapture God's heart and reach peoples of all nations with the good news of Jesus Christ. The Missions Course introduces the concept of the golden thread. The golden thread traces God's story of reconciling and redeeming rebellious humanity from Genesis to Revelation. God's redemptive story culminates in Christ's death, resurrection, and ascension.

In between Jesus' resurrection and ascension, He gives the church a specific mission found in Matthew 28:18-20.

> Jesus came near and said to them, "All authority has been given to me in heaven and on earth. Go, therefore, and make disciples of all nations, baptizing them in the name of the Father and of the Son and of the Holy Spirit, teaching them to observe everything I have commanded you. And remember, I am with you always, to the end of the age."

It is important to include verse 18 of Matthew chapter 28. Blain Eldredge[7], author of *The Paradise King*, describes the human problem as sin, death, and spiritual oppression. Matthew 28:18 reveals Jesus' victory over sin, death, and the forces of spiritual oppression, and now all authority has been given to Him. "Jesus came near and said to them, "All authority has been given to me in heaven and on earth" (Matthew 28:18, CSB). Jesus, the one with all power and authority, conveys a mission to His followers, his church—to go into all the nations and testify that He is the true Savior and King. We see the same scene captured from a different perspective in Acts 1:8-9. During this current season in God's story, the church has the mission of testifying to the gospel, the good news that Jesus is Savior and King of the world. The collective purpose of all Jesus' followers is to invite people to become followers of Jesus and teach them to live Jesus' way.

Inviting people to follow Jesus highlights the collective purpose of the church and is commonly known as evangelism or sharing your faith. Our part in the collective purpose of the church is personal evangelism. Yet, most non-Christians around the world do not personally know a Christian. Even among non-Christians in the United States, 1 in 5 adults do not have a relationship with a Christian[22]. Paul describes the collective purpose of the church in 2 Corinthians 5:19 as being wrapped up in God's mission of reconciling people back to Himself through Christ Jesus. Later in this book, we will discuss the relationship between personal evangelism and leading change in the church.

The Rod – Leading with Principles

Leading with principles is rooted in the reality that everyone is subject to mission drift. Mission drift occurs when one loses focus on one's core identity and purpose[15]. Mission drift can affect us all. Each person has a core identity and purpose (Ephesians 2:10; Romans 8:28-30). The goal of leading with principles is to help those we serve remain focused on who they are and what their kingdom calling.

Paul was very aware of the propensity of followers of Jesus to lose focus on their identity and calling. In 1 Corinthians 9:24-27, Paul urges Christians to discipline themselves to run the race of their faith to win the prize. Paul demonstrates his focus in Philippians chapter 3:

> Brothers and sisters, I do not consider myself to have taken hold of it. But one thing I do: Forgetting what is behind and reaching forward to what is ahead, I pursue as my goal the prize

promised by God's heavenly call in Christ Jesus (Philippians 3:13-14, CSB).

In writing to Timothy, in 2 Timothy chapter 2, Paul urges Timothy to develop a community to help in the ministry and to keep his focus, especially when difficulties arise.

> Share in suffering as a good soldier of Christ Jesus. No one serving as a soldier gets entangled in the concerns of civilian life; he seeks to please the commanding officer. Also, if anyone competes as an athlete, he is not crowned unless he competes according to the rules (2 Timothy 3-5).

Leading with principles was essential in the early church. Today, in the busyness of our world, it can be difficult to maintain our identity and purpose. Adding to the busyness is the onslaught of digital information invading our personal spaces, fighting for our attention, and discouraging, distracting, and derailing us from living a life worthy of our calling (Ephesians 4:1).

The aim of leading with principles is to steward a constructive environment for human flourishing. Human flourishing is a current topic among a variety of disciplines. The Global Flourishing Study identified relationships, character, and purpose as three core components of human flourishing[32]. Biblically, "flourishing" means a person is in an environment where they grow and develop their identity and calling. (Identity and calling are major themes of leading with the process and the next chapter). The

word peace or shalom in the Bible carries the same idea as
flourishing. Therefore, the aim of leading with principles is
tending to the peace or shalom of the environment of those
we serve.

The metaphor from shepherding for leading with
principles is the shepherd's rod. While the shepherd's staff
guides the flock, the rod protects the flock. The shepherd
would use the rod to protect the flock in two ways. First, to
keep the sheep together. The sheep can over-focus on the
grass and the ground right before them. In my late twenties,
I spent the better part of a year on a working sheep ranch in
the Beartooth Mountains in Montana. Too often, I would be
chasing sheep that wandered from the herd, knowing that
if they fell into a ditch, I wouldn't be able to get them out
without considerable help. For those we serve, distractions
come easily. The pace of life often keeps us disconnected.
We lead with principles by coaching and guiding people to
remain connected with others and focused on their identity
and calling rather than becoming discouraged or pursuing
distractions. The second use for the rod is protection. While
I never had to fight off a predator on the ranch in Montana,
the shepherd's rod is traditionally known as a formidable
weapon to defend the flock. Outside attacks can come from
all directions, seeking to derail those in our care. "Be sober-
minded, be alert. Your adversary the devil is prowling
around like a roaring lion, looking for anyone he can
devour" (1 Peter 5:8). Likewise, for those we serve, leading
with principles can protect them from outside attacks that
would seek to derail people from flourishing in their faith
and their identity, and calling in Christ.

Protecting those we serve from distraction and derailment is at the heart of leading with principles. In the post-Christian world of Western culture, filled with diminishing concern for life, oppositional values, and those leaving the Christian church or deconstructing their faith, it may seem easy to become discouraged. Paul knew that followers of Jesus were prone to becoming discouraged. In Philippians 1:9-10, Paul prays for Jesus' followers, "And I pray this: that your love will keep on growing in knowledge and every kind of discernment, so that you may approve the things that are superior and may be pure and blameless in the day of Christ." Galatians 6:9 encourages Christians not to give in to discouragement, "Let us not get tired of doing good, for we will reap at the proper time if we don't give up." Left on our own, we can easily become discouraged. Shepherding Leadership rallies people toward a common mission and helps people remain connected and encouraged to live sent together.

Protecting people from distractions begins with not adding to the busyness of life through over-programming. The goal of shepherding people is not that they will be good enough but that they will flourish with their identity and calling, rooting in the Lord Jesus Christ. Jim Collins[23], in *Good to Great*, describes being good enough as the greatest barrier to becoming great. Being good can become a distraction from being great. Hebrews 13:17 challenges us to follow our leaders since they are accountable to God for how they watch over the souls of those they serve. I cannot think of a better picture of leading with principles than to keep watch over the identity and calling of those we serve. The Apostle Peter expands the beautiful picture of shepherding leadership and leading through principles. "Shepherd God's flock among you, not overseeing out of compulsion but willingly, as God would have you; not out of greed for money but eagerly; not lording it over those entrusted to you, but being examples to the flock (1 Peter 5:2-3, CSB). We protect the people we serve from being distracted, even by the good or good enough, and help them pursue their identity and calling in Jesus Christ.

Leading with principles also involves protecting the people we serve from being derailed. Although the people we serve are often derailed by surrendering themselves to the works of the flesh (Galatians 5:19), we must also protect people from false teachers and false doctrine. As Western culture continues to grow increasingly post-Christian, leading with principles seeks to protect people from the voices, blogs, podcasts, Snappers, TikTokers, and Youtubers that would derail their identity and calling in Christ. The threat of derailment is growing far beyond the voices of the de-churched, exvangelicals, and those deconstructing their faith. During the writing of this book, a large movement was growing in the Global South. The growing movement is larger than prosperity doctrine or Christian nationalism— the New Apostolic Reformation. Paul warns the Ephesian elders in Acts chapter 20:

> I know that after my departure, savage wolves will come in among you, not sparing the flock. Men will rise up even from your own number and distort the truth to lure the disciples into following them. Therefore be on the alert, remembering that night and day for three years

I never stopped warning each one of you with
tears (Acts 20:29-31, CSB).

In the same way, Peter (1 Peter 5:8) and James (James 4:7)
warn that, though they are defeated, forces of spiritual
opposition seek to derail Jesus' followers. Leading with
principles helps those we serve to identify and resist the
adversary of our faith who seeks to derail the flourishing
of Jesus' followers (John 10:10). Leading with purpose
helps people grow in their identity and calling, and leading
with principles protects people from being discouraged,
derailed, or distracted, keeping them on the path of
flourishing, fully deployed in their calling.

The Shepherd's Heart-Leading With Process.

Leading with process is central to Shepherding Leadership.
Leading with process is about creating systems for
equipping, empowering, and releasing people into their
unique calling as they engage with God in His mission.
Leading with process may feel familiar for many church
leaders. Most pastoral training, conferences, and books
target spiritual growth, discipleship, disciple-making,
Christian education, and spiritual formation. While leading
with process does not define the content of a discipleship
pathway or spiritual formation plan, it does declare the
usefulness of a disciplemaking process, which provides
the functional outcomes of equipping, empowering, and
releasing in missional activity.

Shepherding Leadership focuses on how we lead.
Therefore, leading with process focuses on implementing
a disciplemaking process committed to equipping,

empowering, and releasing those we serve. Spiritual
formation or a discipleship pathway is common among the
various Christian traditions. As a result, a significant library
of literature exists, providing content for a disciplemaking
process. Many books have been written on the content,
development, and implementation of a discipleship
pathway, including *What Does it Mean to Follow Jesus* by
Tim Wiebe[24], *The Complete Book of Discipleship* by Bill Hull[25],
Discipleship Essentials by Greg Ogden[26], *real-life discipleship*
by Jim Putman[27], *Multiply* by Frances Chan[28], *Emotionally
Healthy Discipleship* by Peter Scazzero[29], and *Practicing The
Way* by John Mark Comer[30] to name a few. As a dimension
of Shepherding Leadership, leading with the process does
not seek to add content but to drive a disciplemaking
process committed to equipping, empowering, and
releasing the people we lead.

In his second letter to Timothy, Paul declares God's
Word's nature, content, and purpose. "All Scripture is
inspired by God and is profitable for teaching, for rebuking,
for correcting, for training in righteousness, so that the man
of God may be complete, equipped for every good work (2
Timothy 3:16, CSB). 2 Timothy 3:16 is often used to spotlight
the nature of the Scriptures as being inspired by God. 2
Timothy 3:16 also provides a purposeful structure for how
we can use the content of God's Word can be daily. God's
Word helps us learn our identity and purpose (Galatians
2:20) and confronts our thinking and actions when we
choose to live our way instead of God's way (2 Timothy 3;
James 4:17). God's Word helps us align our lives with God's
way (Galatians 5:22-23) and trains or equips us for future
good works (Ephesian 2:10, 4:11-15). Finally, 2 Timothy 3:16

describes the functional outcome of God's Word working in our lives—equipped, empowered, and released to every good work.

Leading with process uses the shepherd metaphor of the shepherd's heart. In John 10, Jesus directs the shepherd metaphor at himself, revealing His heart—His love for us. A great definition of love is the unwavering commitment to the flourishing of another human being[31]. Jesus models an unwavering commitment to the flourishing of humanity through sacrificial service. Using the shepherd metaphor, Jesus models serving the gospel mission and the people. In Shepherding Leadership, we lead with process with a shepherd's heart. The shepherd's heart is committed to serving God's purpose or mission for the church. Through words and actions, the shepherd's heart is committed to testifying that Jesus alone is both Savior and King of all. The shepherd's heart is also committed to serving those we lead. Through leading with process, the Shepherding leader displays an unwavering commitment to the flourishing of those they serve by leading with a disciplemaking process, committed to equipping, empowering, and releasing people to join God in His mission.

The shepherd's heart drives us to lead with process, leveraging our tools for spiritual formation or a discipleship pathway to equip and empower people to flourish in their identity and releasing them into their calling. Often, in the Western Christianity of the Global North, our discipleship pathways, Christian education, and spiritual formation efforts focus on developing one's identity in Christ, maturing Christian behavior, gaining knowledge, and navigating life's challenges. It is easier to prepare a sermon, find a book, or teach a lesson addressing the current needs of marriages, families, parenting, self-esteem, emotional distress, and challenges thrown at us in a culture desperate to deny the reality of a good and loving God. All these challenges are real; the hurt is real, and the anxiety, the stress, and the brokenness are real. While mentoring, coaching, and disciple-making of fellow Christ followers will always need to address our real challenges, leading with process emphasizes one's unique calling or role in God's gospel story. Focusing on calling enables the functional outcomes of our disciplemaking process to address the foundation of what it means to be humans adopted through Christ into God's family, equipped, empowered, and released for God's mission.

Leading with process is an empowering multiplying approach that intersects our spiritual formation plans or discipleship pathways with the biblical commands to engage with Jesus in His mission. As our identity in Christ grows, we begin to discover God's purpose for the church. At this point in our discipleship journey, we need to learn how we, as individuals, fit together into the collective purpose. We recognize our calling once we discover our role within God's redemptive story. The next chapter contains a more in-depth discussion on developing calling and how we release those we serve into their calling. "For we are his workmanship, created in Christ Jesus for good works, which God prepared ahead of time for us to do" (Ephesians 2:10, CSB). Leading with process allows the shepherd's heart to multiply and to be an example for those within our care. The shepherd's heart surfaces concern and compassion among group members, calling everyone into accountability to the collective purpose of the church and empowering the group and individuals toward fulfilling their calling.

Paul championed empowering and releasing people into identity and calling.

> What then is Apollos? What is Paul? They are servants through whom you believed, and each has the role the Lord has given. I planted, Apollos watered, but God gave the growth. So, then, neither the one who plants nor the one who waters is anything, but only God who gives the growth. Now he who plants and he who waters are one, and each will receive his own reward according to his own labor. For we are God's coworkers. You are God's field, God's building (1 Corinthians 3:5-9, CSB).

Paul knew he had a specific role in God's redemptive story, and others had their roles. Each person fits into the larger collective mission of the church—to proclaim Jesus as Savior and King and to multiply disciplemakers.

People cannot engage in their calling to serve their King, Jesus unless empowered and released. Yet empowering and releasing does not look like a mother owl launching her owlets out of the nest where some thrive and others do not. Instead, leading with process continues beyond the release. Paul reminds Timothy that he will need to continue to remember his training and his calling (1 Timothy 1:6). Because we all need ongoing encouragement as we live sent together, helping people live sent on mission with Jesus can be difficult, but release we must! Jesus has given people to build up the church (Ephesians 4:11-12), and God has given Christians gifts to use throughout the fellowship of believers and the communities in which they live (Romans 12:6-8). Like Paul and Peter, the Shepherding Leader must champion releasing others into their calling, into living sent.

> Just as each one has received a gift, use it to serve others as good stewards of the varied grace of God. If anyone speaks, let it be as one who speaks God's words; if anyone serves, let it be from the strength God provides, so that God may be glorified through Jesus Christ in everything. To him be the glory and the power forever and ever. Amen (1 Peter 4:10-11, CSB).

Changing the Way We Lead

Leadership isn't easy. Changing the way we think about leadership will be challenging. Yet, if the church is going to revive, we must change how we lead. The Ecclesia-motus framework provides a picture or model for refocusing our vision of the church as a multiplying movement. Not mini movements focused on an individual or idea, movements that pop up for a season and then fade—instead, mobilizing the entire capital "C" church as a multiplying movement for Jesus, our King. To get there, we will need to be fully committed to the collective purpose of the church. The Great Commission isn't a verse for foreign or local missions and missionaries. The Great Commission is the collective purpose of the Church, of every follower of Jesus. As leaders within the church, we need to be sold out on equipping, empowering, and releasing people into their calling and their unique role in God's grand, amazing, and mysterious redemptive story. Shepherding Leadership's staff keeps the focus on our collective gospel-driven purpose. The shepherd's rod protects people from being discouraged, distracted, or derailed as they live sent together with their king. The shepherd's heart seeks to serve the mission and to serve people, equipping, empowering, and releasing people into the multiplying movement of the kingdom of God.

You may be thinking, "I've heard all this before," and yes, hopefully you have. To revive, the church must revive, but it is not a tear-the-whole-thing-down-and-start-over sort of change. The change needed in the church is more like a renovation. Too many people spend too much time tearing down the Church of the Living God. We need change that builds the church, that revives and revitalizes the church. In the next chapter, we will explore beyond the way we lead and hopefully glimpse how revitalizing change might look.

CHAPTER 5 – END NOTES

1. Routledge, R. (2010). Did God Create Chaos? Unresolved Tension in Genesis 1:1-2. *Tyndale Bulletin, 61*(1), 69–88. https://doi.org/10.53751/001c.29296

2. Heiser, M. S. (2019). *The Unseen Realm: Recovering the Supernatural Worldview of the Bible* (Reprint edition). Lexham Press.

3. Phillips, R. D. (2016). *The Masculine Mandate: God's Calling to Men.* Ligonier Ministries.

4. Cole, T. (2017, July 24). God Didn't Create Us to be Farmers: Genesis 2:15 [Blog]. *Redeemer Bible Church.* https://redeemerbible.org/blog-1/2017/7/24/god-didnt-create-us-to-be-farmers-genesis-215

5. Heiser, M. (2015). Supernatural: What the Bible Teaches about the Unseen World and Why It Matters. Lexham Press.

6. Schrock, D., Pelt, M. V. V., & Ortlund, D. (2022). *The Royal Priesthood and the Glory of God.* Crossway.

7. Eldredge, B. (2023). *The Paradise King: The Tragic History and Spectacular Future of Everything According to Jesus of Nazareth.* Blaine Eldredge.

8. By, R. T. (2021). Leadership: In Pursuit of Purpose. *Journal of Change Management, 21*(1), 30–44. https://doi.org/10.1080/14697017.2021.1861698

9. Rost, J. C. (1993). Leadership development in the new millennium. *Journal of Leadership Studies, 1*(1), 91–110. https://doi.org/10.1177/107179199300100109

10. Greenleaf, R. K. (1970). *The servant as leader (an essay)*. Greenleaf Organization.

11. Leman, K., & Pentak, W. (2004). *The Way of the Shepherd: Seven Secrets to Managing Productive People* (1st edition). Zondervan.

12. Kinnaman, D., Matlock, M., & Hawkins, A. (2019). *Faith for exiles: 5 ways for a new generation to follow Jesus in digital Babylon*. Baker Books.

13. Storm, A. (2023, June 21). Principles of Andragogy: Theory, Examples, and Implementation. *Thinkific*. https://www.thinkific.com/blog/principles-andragogy/

14. Levey, N. (2024, September 17). These factory workers were swamped by medical debt. Then their employer stepped in. *NPR*. https://www.npr.org/2024/09/17/nx-s1-5100642/medical-debt-solution-free-primary-care

15. Greer, P., Horst, C., Haggard, A., & Crouch, A. (2015). *Mission Drift: The Unspoken Crisis Facing Leaders, Charities, and Churches* (Reprint edition). Bethany House Publishers.

16. Lencioni, P. M. (2002). *The Five Dysfunctions of a Team: A Leadership Fable, 20th Anniversary Edition* (1st edition). Jossey-Bass.

17. Lencioni, P. M. (2012). *The Advantage: Why Organizational Health Trumps Everything Else In Business* (1st edition). Jossey-Bass.

18. Collins, J. (2001). *Good to Great: Why Some Companies Make the Leap... And Others Don't* (First Edition). Harper Business.

19. Kotter, J. P. (2012). *Leading Change, With a New Preface by the Author* (1R edition). Harvard Business Review Press.

20. Mancini, W. (2010). *Church unique: How missional leaders cast vision, capture culture, and create movement.* John Wiley & Sons.

21. *The Missions Course | A 6-Week Study on God's Heart for The Nations.* (n.d.). Retrieved December 17, 2024, from https://themissionscourse.com/

22. Alper, G. A. S., Patricia Tevington, Justin Nortey, Michael Rotolo, Asta Kallo and Becka A. (2024, January 24). Religious 'Nones' in America: Who They Are and What They Believe. *Pew Research Center.* https://www.pewresearch.org/religion/2024/01/24/religious-nones-in-america-who-they-are-and-what-they-believe/

23. Collins, J. (2001). *Good to Great: Why Some Companies Make the Leap... And Others Don't* (First Edition). Harper Business.

24. Wiebe, T. (2024). *What Does It Mean to Follow Jesus?: A Clear, Biblical Picture of Discipleship.* Independently published.

25. Hull, B. (2006). *The Complete Book of Discipleship: On Being and Making Followers of Christ* (Annotated edition). NavPress.

26. Ogden, G. (2019). *Discipleship Essentials: A Guide to Building Your Life in Christ* (Revised, Revised and Expanded edition). IVP.

27. Putman, J. (2010). *Real-Life Discipleship: Building Churches That Make Disciples*. NavPress.

28. Chan, F., & Beuving, M. (2012). *Multiply: Disciples Making Disciples* (First Edition). David C Cook.

29. Scazzero, P. (2021). *Emotionally Healthy Discipleship: Moving from Shallow Christianity to Deep Transformation*. Zondervan.

30. Comer, J. M. (2024). *Practicing the Way: Be with Jesus. Become like him. Do as he did.* WaterBrook.

31. Buckingham, M. (2022). *Love and Work: How to Find What You Love, Love What You Do, and Do It for the Rest of Your Life*. Harvard Business Review Press.

32. Padgett, R. N., Cowden, R. G., Chattopadhyay, M., Han, Y., Honohan, J., Ritter, Z., Srinivasan, R., Johnson, B. R., & VanderWeele, T. J. (2025). Survey sampling design in wave 1 of the Global Flourishing Study. *European Journal of Epidemiology*. https://doi.org/10.1007/s10654-024-01167-9

CHAPTER 6

CALLING AND CARING

Whatever you do, do it from the heart, as something done for the Lord and not for people, knowing that you will receive the reward of an inheritance from the Lord. You serve the Lord Christ.
Colossians 3:23-24 (CSB)

Work is our design and dignity; it is also a way to serve God through creativity, particularly in creating culture.
Timothy Keller

Bad Form

In my early 20's, I suffered from a nagging elbow injury. Cycling and mountain biking were among my favorite outdoor activities growing up in the Pacific Northwest. My daily rides would take me through lush, wooded forests or clearings with glimpses of the Cascade Mountains to the north or Mount Rainier to the south. I would ride through rolling foothills, past lakes, alongside rivers, and each day, I could choose from various challenging hill climbs. My everyday rides were amazing, challenging, and bad for me.

It wasn't the routes, the terrain, or the hill climbs that were bad for me. It wasn't even that I was riding. I was, to date, in the best shape of my life. What hurt me while out on my bicycle was my form.

I never had a fitting for the bicycle I was riding. The result was bad form. My bad form was straining away at the tendons in my elbows, forming tendinitis. The immediate solution was to rest my elbows, but the long-term solution was to fix my form. So, like any other twenty-year-old male, I ignored the resting advice, was fitted for my bicycle, and began focusing on my form. Guess what? It worked! Eventually, my elbows healed, and the pain vanished. It wasn't cycling or mountain biking hurting me; it was my form. Sometimes, significant change can happen from simply changing your form.

To revive the church, we must change our form. The change in form needed to change the church orbits around how we engage in calling. In a world of people frantically trying to find their purpose, redefining themselves to fit someone else's purpose, or seeking to escape the discomfort of not knowing their purpose, the church has an opportunity to help people flourish. In his book *Working*, Stud Terkel[1] draws two important truths about human beings from the stories of many different people: we all have a degree of ambition, and each seeks significance. Children in Western culture are raised with an ethos of self-determination. Many parents provide their children with opportunities while limiting exposure to failing. Unfortunately, even in Christian circles, the concept of discovering our calling is broken. Calling is reserved for the few, specifically calling into missions or vocational ministry.

Many people work jobs without calling; their purpose is to pay bills. Engaging in God's gospel mission happens outside work hours, often competing with family life and recreational opportunities. Our calling form is off. We no longer expect day laborers like fishermen, activists like the Zealots, or office workers like tax collectors to be called into Jesus' kingdom mission. As a result, people find their identity in their occupation and their significance in their work. Leaving little time and energy for their kingdom calling.

Calling among Christians and non-Christians often involves discussions about aptitudes, strengths, and passions with the goal of a palatable and potentially profitable career. Human ambition rules over calling, setting up an impossible-to-win battle where we wield our efforts to gain significance. Merriam-Webster's dictionary defines ambition as a desire for a specific end, or status and control[2]. Significance in Christian circles often equates to one's sense of worth or identity[3]. Modern Western culture celebrates ambition and anxiously pursues significance. Instead of significance and ambition, God created humans to embrace their identity and calling. God created humans and called us to participate in His purpose or mission. In Genesis 1:28, God gave humanity a purpose and agency—the motivation or ambition to participate with God in His mission. The human bent for significance is answered through spiritual formation or discipleship, helping people understand and receive their identity from God through His presence and declarations throughout the Bible. A biblical worldview reframes ambition as usefulness for calling. In many of his letters, Paul speaks of the partnership of others and, specifically, highlights the usefulness of Onesimus and John Mark. Paul also speaks of his ambition for God's mission, "But my life is worth nothing to me unless I use it for finishing the work assigned me by the Lord Jesus—the work of telling others the Good News about the wonderful grace of God" (Acts 20:24, NLT). Terkel chronicles the tales of many who feel their occupations are too small to win their identity or declare them significant. We need to correct our form. We need to address the role of calling, of each person's calling, in the church.

Calling

Calling is an interesting topic. Most theologians believe that we have primary and secondary callings. The easily agreed upon primary calling is to have a personal relationship with God through the life, death, resurrection, and ascension of Jesus Christ. The secondary callings are more complex. Are we called to be part of a local church? Are we to engage in the mission of the church? Are we called to use our gifts to serve others? Are we called to make a positive contribution to the world? Are we called to a specific career path? Separating our calling to follow Jesus and our calling to live with Jesus is a Western error, separating the sacred from the secular. The core to understanding human dignity and worth is that humans are created with and for a purpose or calling. Calling is part of being fully human. Calling affects identity, yet some people resist God's invitation to be reconciled through Jesus and still strive to live out their calling. Our identity changes as we respond to God's invitation to be in a relationship with Him through Jesus.

REVIVE   154

Calling and identity are intimately connected, whether we resist or respond.

Calling is an essential aspect of what it means to be human. God has chosen to weave into His great story each human as an essential character. We yield to God's sovereign design, knowing God is the agent of our identity and calling. Because our identity and our calling are informed externally by God and internally by our personal histories (interests, desires, and experiences), we cannot simply take a test to know our calling. Likewise, we cannot assume our calling is not unique and generally informed by a passage of scripture. God has created humans as relational beings (Genesis 2:18), and we discover our calling, preferably in relationship with God and others. In Ephesians 2:10, Paul declares that each of us, each human, is a masterpiece of God.

Each human has dignity, value, and purpose. "For we are his workmanship, created in Christ Jesus for good works, which God prepared ahead of time for us to do" (Ephesians 2:10, CSB). The Greek word used for workmanship is poēma. From poēma, we have the English words for poem and poetry. The basic definition of poēma is to make something. Building on the basic definition of poēma, we understand that poēma is an artistic making—a creation of art and beauty! Each human life is a poem God is writing. Every day, when you wake up, God is forming your day as His poetry. God's Great Story is an epic tale of many poems, like the Iliad. God's epic tale comprises the poems of each of His followers. Every character in God's story is important. In God's story of redemption, the Author enters the story and engages with each character, developing and revealing their uniqueness, the art and beauty of God's creative work. Therefore, calling isn't left in the realm of only what is accomplished in God's story; calling is God's direct involvement with each character in His epic poem.

Regaining Our Calling

When humanity rebelled against God, shalom, or peace, was broken. Amy Sherman[4] introduces a four-fold understanding of shalom or peace. The four aspects of shalom are four areas in which peace is necessary for human flourishing. Our understanding of shalom can be broken down into our relationship with God, our relationship with self, our relationship with others, and our relationship with creation. In Genesis 2:15, God places humans in the garden and gives them a purpose—responsibility over creation. Humans were not made for broken peace, broken shalom. Even humans, convinced there is no God, strive to find purpose in life. Trapped inside a concentration camp in World War II, Victor Frankl[5] discovered that humans need a purpose to flourish. Frankl observed that humans find purpose or meaning in life through work, love, and suffering. Ambition is part of the human experience, yet our effort and results alone do not provide a sense of well-being, hinting that something is wrong.

Broken shalom is broken peace with God. Here, the theologian's primary and secondary callings make sense. Because we cannot fix our broken shalom on our own. We need God to fix it for us through Jesus Christ. People try to fix broken shalom all the time. Religion and works-based salvation are a human attempt to fix our broken peace with God. Self-help, the workout revolution, and New Year's resolutions are all human attempts to fix shalom. People attempt to fix broken shalom with one another, which erupts as conflicts, wars, lawsuits, racial tension, and injustice. People seek to fulfill their broken shalom with creation by defining their calling or purpose around themselves or a cause. Yet, without a restored relationship with God and reconnection to God and His purpose, our identity, relationships, and calling will always be anchored to self-interest and self-survival.

Broken shalom is more than a spiritual concern. Shalom embodies four interconnected dimensions: peace with God or spirituality, peace with ourselves or mental well-being, peace with others or a just societal flourishing, and peace with the created order or purpose and beauty. There is only one solution for broken shalom, one payment for our sin, and only one who could restore shalom. Jesus Christ, fully God and fully human, is the restorer of shalom through his life, death, resurrection, and ascension. In God's redemptive story, Jesus has called his followers to live out their roles or callings. Broken shalom and calling are connected. Human ambition is rooted in a desire to be useful. Restored shalom leads us to true usefulness—to embrace our calling.

Calling is a vast subject. Purpose, role, and ability to work are the big rocks defining one's calling. What is God's purpose? How has God designed, impassioned, and directed me in His story, and where and when can I live out my role? Can a simple framework identifying God's purpose for our lives, revealing our role within

God's purpose, and mobilizing us on mission help identify our calling in God's kingdom? Three basic questions unearth the big rocks of calling: Why me? Why here? Why now? The questions are simple, but the answers are not necessarily easy. There are many trails to hike in the Rocky Mountains. Many of the trails are very simple to follow, but making the ascent of a 12,500ft pass is not easy. Yet, the difficult climb up the mountain to identify your calling is possible in the right environment, with the right people around you. If the church is going to revive, we need to adjust our form. We must go from viewing calling as only for the few to embracing calling for every follower of Jesus. Every Christian can be useful for the kingdom. As leaders in the church, Jesus' kingdom mission is of the utmost importance; the kingdom calling of every believer is next. Calling intimately connects to our following. As leaders, helping others discover God's purpose for their life, their calling or role in God's redemptive story, and empowering and releasing them in their calling is real leadership.

Calling and Caring

It wasn't until later in life, after I moved to the woods of Minnesota and Wisconsin, traveled the corn fields of the mid-west, and through the rolling Tennessee mountains, that I realized I grew up in a forest. Our small subdivision just east of Seattle was surrounded by trees with large trunks and sturdy branches. Even in the regular Seattle rains, the canopy of the towering pines kept us and the forest floor of soft pine needles dry. Stories like *Swiss Family Robinson* and *My Side of the Mountain* captured my imagination because I believed, as a nine-year-old outdoorsman, I could carve out a life in the woods. I missed curfew more than once, having climbed stories above the rooftops with fellow explorers, misjudging how long it would take to climb down in the fading light of sunset. No one ever taught me how to play in the forest. I was told to go outside and play, so I did. For some of us, we find our calling the same way. Someone tells us that God created us on purpose for His purpose—'go outside and find your calling.' And we do. My son didn't grow up in a forest or a place safe enough for him to wander without boundaries. The growing number and volume of voices declaring the importance of oneself compete for his and our attention. I am watching as my son travels into early adulthood, yearning to discover who God has created him to be. Yet, it will be difficult for him to discover his calling in a culture that demands he be significant. It is difficult for many to figure out what they want out of life, even more so to discern our calling in God's Great Story.

Jesus' body, the faith family we call the local church, and we, as leaders, have an opportunity to help the next generation respond to the gospel call to salvation and the call of God's kingdom mission. We have an opportunity to help the next generation discover and engage in their kingdom calling. If the church is going to revive, we need to re-envision our roles as leaders. The upcoming generations need their leaders to be coaches of calling, equippers of identity, and releasers in the kingdom's mission.

Each of our kingdom callings begins with being called to our King. At the beginning of our journey, we are broken and selfish. Brandon Eldridge[6] described the problem for every human at the beginning of their life as a

problem with death, sin, and forces of spiritual oppression.
Death because our bodies are mortal, temporary. Sin
because we are a race that has rebelled against God, and
if anyone would question this reality, they only need to
examine their past twenty-four hours to provide proof to
Romans 3:23. I cannot argue with the forces of spiritual
oppression since they are clearly seen as the gods of this
world throughout human history. In Colossians chapter
2, Paul explains how Jesus is God's solution for all three
problems- death, sin, and darkness.

> For you were buried with Christ when you were
> baptized. And with him, you were raised to new
> life because you trusted the mighty power of
> God, who raised Christ from the dead. You were
> dead because of your sins and because your
> sinful nature was not yet cut away. Then God
> made you alive with Christ, for he forgave all
> our sins (Colossians 2:12-13, CSB).

Through Jesus, God fixes our brokenness. God, by His
grace, makes us alive with Christ. Because of Christ's
finished work, God forgives all our sins. In verse fifteen,
God disarms the spiritual powers, and in verse twenty, he
sets us free from the spiritual powers of this world. God
did all of this by His grace for us through Jesus Christ.
As undeserving recipients of God's grace, we are driven
toward Colossians 3:2, "Think about the things of heaven,
not the things of earth: (CSB). But, before our focus is
enraptured with things of heaven, before we lead and help

people discover and live their calling, we begin our journey broken and selfish.

As we journey forward into discovering and living our kingdom calling, we carry baggage. Some of the bags we carry we have packed ourselves. We neatly pack our bags with desires of significance, financial expectations, relationship expectations, consequences of decisions, passions, hobbies, skills, anxieties, fears, and dreams. Too often, unmet expectations, trauma, and even other people help pack the baggage we carry. Our families of origin, culture, siblings, parents, teachers, coaches, pastors, and ministry leaders join the chorus, helping us pack our bags. The truth is that we care about what is in our bags. And some of the contents of our bags teach us to care for others (2 Corinthians 1:3-4). The contents of our bags often inform the objects of our caring and guide us toward living our missional calling in a disciplemaking process. As we discover our identity in Christ, how God has fashioned us to care about people and problems, and how God calls us daily to engage in His kingdom mission, we will learn to connect our calling to what we care about. As we learn to walk with God, God breaks our hearts for what breaks His heart at the intersections of our calling and caring. Understanding the intersection of what we care about and God's kingdom calling helps identify our daily role in God's gospel mission.

Leading with process engages people in a spiritual formation plan or discipleship pathway, developing identity in Christ and clarifying kingdom calling. Shepherding Leadership invites us to learn the stories of those we serve. As we learn their stories and what they care

about, we can coach them toward connecting their calling
and their caring. Many great resources exist to help lead
people in a spiritual formation plan or a discipleship
pathway. Different denominations and church traditions
offer varying and unique approaches. The goal of this book
is to realign and revitalize our determination to develop
people's identity in Christ, their kingdom calling, and
release them to engage daily in God's kingdom mission.
Every resource or approach should be evaluated and used
only if the goals of identity, calling, and missional
engagement are supported.

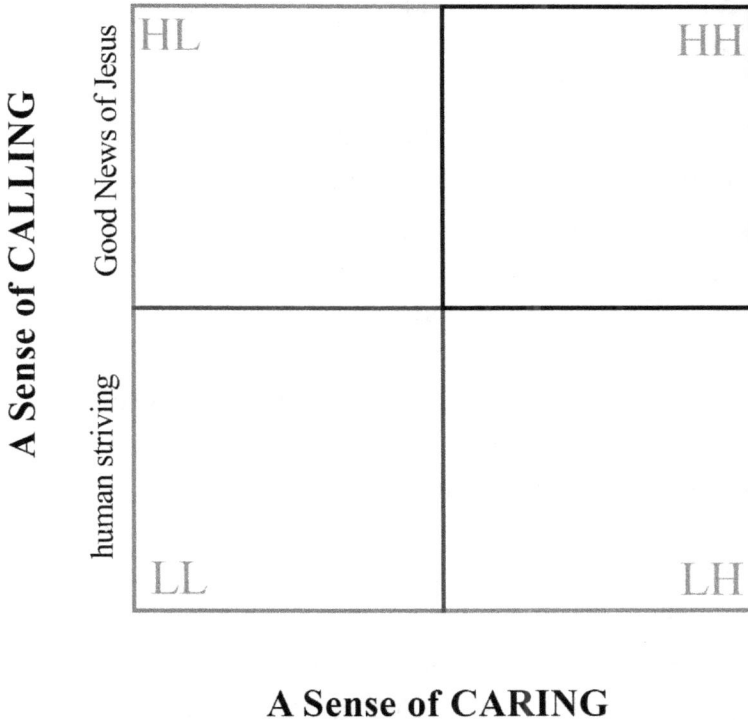

A Sense of CARING

The Calling and Caring framework was created to assist a spiritual formation plan or discipleship pathway, helping to connect one's calling and caring and mobilizing people into daily missional movement. The Calling and Caring framework is a standard two-by-two grid with low-low, low-high, high-low, and high-high quadrants to visualize the connection between Calling and Caring. Common sense informs us that humans are not perfect and that purpose or usefulness is essential to human flourishing. Calling and Caring become two competing yet connected human desires. Using the Calling and Caring framework, we can visualize our journey from broken and selfish to people empowered, equipped, and released into daily missional movement.

In the Calling and Caring framework, Calling focuses on our need for shalom and to be mentally, spiritually, and emotionally whole—our caring combines our personal histories with our desire for usefulness or purpose in our daily lives. The recognition and responsibility of our sin and rebellion against the Most High God is part of being Committed to Calling—as God invites us to surrender to Jesus and receive His salvation. In this sense, my calling is turning from living life my way (Repenting of my sin, which has broken shalom in my life) and submitting to living life God's way—a way of life where I seek to walk in restored shalom.

Committed to Calling goes beyond my salvation and relationship with Jesus. Committed to Calling also involves being active in the mission God gave to the church—to testify that Jesus is Savior and King through our words and how we serve others. Committed to Calling is connected to Committed to Caring since Jesus did not come to gather people as servants but rather to serve the world's people (Matthew 20:28).

We live in a world where one's religious faith is considered a weakness or evidence of being uneducated. At the same time, helping others is viewed as good. The needed inclusion within the "Establishment" clause of the First Amendment of the United States Constitution keeps the government from establishing a religion. While not specified in the Constitution, this clause has been carried forward as a separation of church and state and used to nullify the good contributions of the church. Today, the United States government provides opportunities to care for many hurting people through various agencies and grants. Yet, many who care for and seek to serve others must keep their faith at bay when working alongside the government. The unfortunate interpretation leading to the separation of church and state further fuels the notion that helping others is good, but religious faith is not, or at least not helpful. For Christians, Committed to Caring means recognizing that my identity in Christ releases me to surrender my life from being all about me and intentionally dedicate my life to uplifting others and pointing them toward Jesus.

The Calling and Caring framework has four quadrants. The bottom left is Low-Low or the "Self-help" quadrant. The bottom right is the Low-High or the "I have the answers" quadrant. The upper left is the High-Low or the "Jesus is my answer" quadrant. The Upper right is the High-High or "Jesus is God's provision" quadrant. The bottom half of the framework, represented by Low-Low and Low-High, encompasses human striving. The top half of the framework, represented by High-Low and High-High, embraces the good news that Jesus is our Savior and King.

"Self-help," in the bottom left, describes someone who is low in calling and caring. The "Self-help" person is spiritually over God[7], meaning they have no need for God in their life. Truth is derived relative to the person or from a humanistic worldview. A person in Low-Low often lives a consumer life, focusing on self, pleasure, and survival (Romans 1). While the "Self-help" quadrant might seem the least desirable of all four, biblically and psychosocially[8], this is where every human begins their journey.

"I have the answers" is in the bottom right describing someone who is high in caring, while remaining low in calling. A person in Low-High is spiritually similar to the "Self-help" person but demonstrates a deep concern for others. The "I have the answers" person is also over God and has no need for God in their life, often ascribing to atheistic, humanistic, or naturalistic worldviews. However, the "I have the answers" person sees the brokenness in the world and, in response, feels they have a responsibility to help. Their caring drives their actions. The "I have the answers" person may also believe they have the answers to solve other's problems or at least be part of the solution. An "I have the answers" person may likely participate in civic work, social work, education, counseling, protesting, or volunteerism.

"Jesus is my answer" quadrant is the upper left describing someone who is high in calling, yet low in caring. Moving to the upper half of the framework, we move from human striving to the acceptance of the gospel. The gospel is simply the good news that Jesus is both Savior and King of the entire world. The "Jesus is my answer" person is spiritually very different than the lower quadrants, recognizing their brokenness, understanding Jesus is God's provision to restore and redeem humanity, surrendering their lives to Jesus, and receiving His salvation. "Jesus is my answer" people have discovered Jesus and surrendered their lives to Him as the only hope for restoration with God, self, others, and creation. While the "Jesus is my answer" quadrant is beneficial, later, we will discuss the challenges of getting stuck here and not moving into the "Jesus is God's provision" quadrant.

"Jesus is God's provision" is the upper right, representing those who pursing their calling in connection with their caring. "Jesus is God's provision" people are committed to joining in God's mission with Him by proclaiming the good news that Jesus is the savior and king and engaging in acts of service reflecting Jesus' kingdom (Isaiah 61:1-2; James 1:27). Spiritually, "Jesus is God's provision" people are active in their following of Jesus, are working through a discipleship pathway, engaging in disciplemaking, encouraging others to engage God's mission, and are becoming multiplying disciplemakers. Note that the people in the "Jesus is God's provision" quadrant have not all arrived, but rather, like Paul, their life aims to be useful for God's mission (Philippians 3:12-14).

Leading People to Calling and Caring

The church must revive. Every follower of Jesus must be equipped, empowered, and released into God's kingdom mission. If the church will revive, we need to correct our form in the area of calling. As leaders, we must embrace calling for everyone, not only those called into vocational ministry. We must recognize that kingdom calling can range from serving in ministry to living mobilized on mission with God each day.

Correcting our form means adopting a new way to lead. Shepherding Leadership serves those we lead, equipping people with their identity in Christ, empowering people in their kingdom calling, and releasing/mobilizing people into their role in God's great story. The cost of living has increased in the United States, and approximately 78% of Americans live paycheck to paycheck[9]. Some may live paycheck to paycheck because of consumer debt, medical bills, or simply because their income is barely sufficient for their lifestyle. Unfortunately, working for a paycheck can take priority over calling. Focusing on making ends meet distracts and derails people from embracing their calling and engaging in their daily role in God's mission. Living only for a paycheck often leaves little spare time to engage in living into our calling and living on a mission. Yet, calling and employment need not compete. We must help those we serve settle for nothing less than embracing their calling amidst their daily work [10]. Calling must be embraced by everyone for the sake of the mission and for the sake of those whose only chance to hear about Jesus is from a coworker.

Adjusting our form to focus on calling requires us to lead with Shepherding Leadership. Shepherding leadership has three aspects, and each aspect has a self-contained metric. First, we help people connect with God and His mission. While connecting with God is an abstract concept, we can measure if we provide accessible opportunities for connecting to God and His mission. When we meet each week, do we regularly talk about God, the good news of Jesus, and the church's mission? We can also formally or informally measure people's perceptions of our offerings. Informally, we can learn people's stories of connecting with God and living on mission with Him. Formally, we can conduct surveys or use a spiritual health report. The form used to help people connect to God and His mission depends on church tradition and denominational forms. Therefore, suggesting a what-to-do approach for leading with Shepherding Leadership would be irresponsible. Instead of what-to-do, the description of Shepherding Leadership uses a how-to approach.

In the first aspect of Shepherding Leadership, we lead with purpose, helping people connect to God and His mission. Many elements of worship services help people connect with God including worship through song and sacrament, teaching, and communing with other Christians. Additionally, our worship services should reinforce the content and commitment to God's mission. Leading with purpose may be best measured through stories of people growing closer to God and engaging with God on mission.

The second aspect is to lead with process. Leading with process helps those we serve grow in their identity as a follower of Jesus and in their ability to engage in God's mission. The metrics of leading with process are simple: are people growing in their identity in Christ and their preparedness for mission? Leading with process cannot stand alone since there is an embedded tension within

the metrics of growth and preparedness. Preparedness
or equipping leads to growth. But growth doesn't lead to
being prepared; growth leads to action. Therefore, we can
only measure one's growth and preparedness by observing
how one lives and engages in God's mission. We must
know our people, not just on Sundays but also Monday
through Saturday. We can only measure leading with
process as we help people mobilize on mission. People
mobilized on mission, create the metric with their stories.
We capture stories of people engaging neighbors and
coworkers, stepping out of their comfort zones, thriving in
the joys and trials of life, and communing with God and
others. We capture stories to measure the influence of our
process.

The final aspect of Shepherding Leadership is
leading with principles. Leading with principles helps those
we lead by protecting them from becoming discouraged,
distracted, or derailed. Group alignment and group attitude
satisfy the metrics for leading with principles. Group
alignment measures if everyone is on the same page. Do
people feel they belong to your church, or do they feel like
an outsider? Do people know and own the church's mission
and values? Are your attendees showing up regularly or
infrequently? Group attitude is measured by asking if those
we serve are being discouraged, distracted, or derailed from
living their identity on daily mission with God? Attitude
can be difficult to measure, so we must be as sensitive to
people's questions and concerns as we are to their victories
and celebrations (Romans 12:15).

Because calling and caring are linked, people will
be released into various types of service. Throughout

the different seasons of ministry with students, I always
surrounded myself with a team of adults who cared for
the needs of the students. Looking back, some seasons of
ministry were more effective than others. During a very
effective season of ministry, I remember saying to a group
of adults that they smelled like student ministry leaders.
Ministry was effective because the adults engaged in their
calling and caring. Other seasons of ministry were less
effective. Since I hadn't recognized the connection between
calling and caring, I thought it was enough that the adults
cared for the students. When the ministry was less effective,
I doubled down on my leadership, not knowing that my
efforts were merely propping up a team of caring adults
whose calling was probably not students. When calling and
caring are linked, God's kingdom advances, whether it's
a ministry of a church, a teacher in a classroom, an office
worker, a truck driver, or an amateur thespian at the local
playhouse. When calling and caring are connected, God's
kingdom mission advances.

As a leader, you are tasked with helping people
discover who God has created them to be, despite, and
sometimes because of, their ups and downs, wins and
losses, wounds and scars. As leaders within a changing
church, our focus is helping people connect with God's
mission and their daily missional role. We help people
connect through pathways that already exist inside each
of them: calling and caring. Engaging people with calling
embodies God's gospel mission, holding the gospel of
Jesus Christ as being of first importance. The Shepherding
Leadership model is essential because calling and caring are
how God wired people to connect with Him[11] and to engage

daily with God in His mission. Shepherding Leadership recognizes that everyone is unique. Each person we serve cares uniquely and has a unique calling. As leaders, we launch or send people to daily roles in God's mission. It is probable that many people willing to serve in their local church are engaged in ministries that discourage, distract, or derail them from engaging daily in God's mission. Since everyone is unique, everyone's calling is unique. Yes, indeed, God often uses groups of people with similar callings within churches, but the people, not a ministry strategy or program, must drive the local church's activities. "Then he said to his disciples, "The harvest is abundant, but the workers are few. Therefore, pray to the Lord of the harvest to send out workers into his harvest" (Matthew 9:37-38, CSB). Our task as leaders is to prepare and send workers into the harvest, not to strategize a better way to bring in the harvest by ourselves.

Leading people to calling and caring is both simple and difficult. Leading people to calling and caring is as simple as adjusting or tweaking our calling form. We begin asking questions about how people connect to God and His mission through your Sunday services. Does your path of discipleship or spiritual formation plan help people grow in their identity in Christ and their ability to engage with God on His mission? Does your disciplemaking strategy mobilize people on mission, releasing them to live sent with God and others daily? Do you protect your people from bad theology and disruptive teachings? Are you ensuring that your people are not distracted by too many good opportunities or ministry programs that they miss the best opportunity of joining God on His mission? As leaders in the church, we may benefit by adopting the perspective of trainers or coaches as we address the need to correct our calling form. Like a trainer or a coach, we know that change is good but often takes intentionality, time, encouragement, and repetition. Change also requires moving through barriers. The Calling and Caring framework can help leaders visualize the barriers people may need to overcome as we coach them toward connecting their calling and their caring in God's mission.

Unstuck and Moving Forward

Kyle Idleman's[12], *not a fan,* addressed the need to adjust our form in how we follow Jesus. We must move from attending church and wearing the title "Christian" toward people who intimately follow Jesus in every part of our lives. Intimately following Jesus should bear fruit—engaging in Jesus-like Holy Spirit filled action. The Shepherding Leader helps people connect calling and caring with the same goal of Jesus-like Holy Spirit-filled action. Idleman addresses the need for individuals to adjust their form in following Jesus. Likewise, the goal of Shepherding Leadership is to adjust calling form, mobilizing entire churches on God's kingdom mission. Shepherding Leadership is the tool that connects calling with caring, helping leaders make the calling form adjustment for themselves and their churches. Therefore, we need to revisit the Calling and Caring framework to discuss moving people from where they are to where they need to grow. The Calling and Caring framework helps identify where people get stuck and the path toward connecting their calling to their caring and being mobilized on mission with God.

The "win" in the Calling and Caring framework is to have people live daily on God's mission, recognizing that Jesus is God's provision for the world. Jesus is our hope, our salvation, and Jesus alone is the source of true life (John 10:10) for today and the age to come. We know that joining in God's mission calls for all of Jesus' followers to engage in personal evangelism, declaring the gospel through words and tangible acts of love. The gospel does not separate the teachings of Jesus from the atoning actions of Jesus. We need to move people toward the high-calling and high-caring quadrant. When people are stuck in high-caring, they lead forth with good actions but no truth. Many people, programs, and agencies are very helpful for those needing food, clothing, housing, education, personal freedom, physical health, mental health, etc. Yet, action without truth, while good, is simply a rescue. It's not that rescuing people is bad, just the opposite. But only rescuing people is not the gospel; it is not God's mission. When people are stuck in the high-calling quadrant, they focus primarily on Jesus Christ as Savior and the only way to have eternal life (John 14:6) and go to Heaven. Yet, truth without action, without love, produces an image of Jesus that is impotent to affect lives here and now. The Church becomes a waiting room for Heaven, and the world a place that is best avoided and ignored. Just proclaiming the truth of Jesus without actions representing His love does not reflect God's mission. We aim to use our spiritual formation plans or discipleship pathways to move people through the Calling and Caring framework so they are mobilized daily in God's mission, living, acting, and proclaiming that Jesus is God's provision for the world.

As people grow and move through the Calling and
Caring framework, there are inherent barriers. Moving
through the barriers requires leading with purpose,
principles, and process, helping us lead people toward
movement. Some barriers represent the need to come
to saving faith in Jesus, growing in sanctification. Yet,
others may function as measurable personal and spiritual
growth indicators, depending on how disciplemaking is
implemented in your context.

The gospel, God's mission, and personal evangelism
are about helping people move out of the "Self-help" or
Low-Low quadrant. Human striving, worldly wisdom,
and personal gain drive the "Self-help" quadrant (James
3:13-16). People living in the Self-help quadrant are stuck
listening to a broken GPS. In the early days of GPS, I
traveled to Purdue, IN, for an EFCA Challenge Student
Conference. The map book and GPS suggested slightly
different routes. The difference in question concerned
a newer bypass verses an older business route. Having
studied the map, I knew the business route was 20 miles
shorter in distance than the bypass. The GPS said otherwise.
In the days before GPS was programmed to reroute
travelers, my GPS told me to return to the route again and
again as we waited in traffic for an extra 30 minutes. It's
one thing to be wrong in front of your wife and family, but
I was in a van full of high schoolers, with three more vans
following me. The fifteen-year-old sitting shotgun revoked
my navigating privileges for the remainder of the trip. No
matter where we are in life, we have a choice between two
distinct and opposing voices. Wisdom that is from God and

Wisdom that is from the world. There is only one escape from earthly wisdom – Jesus.

> And when you were dead in trespasses and in the uncircumcision of your flesh, he made you alive with him and forgave us all our trespasses. He erased the certificate of debt, with its obligations, that was against us and opposed to us, and has taken it away by nailing it to the cross. He disarmed the rulers and authorities and disgraced them publicly; he triumphed over them in him (Colossians 2:13-15, CSB).

Paul describes Jesus' accomplishments on the cross in Colossians chapter 2, verses 13-15. Jesus defeats death, offering humanity new life through the same power that raised Jesus from the dead (Romans 8:10-11). Jesus defeats sin, as Paul describes here in Colossians chapter 2, by erasing our debts and nailing them to the cross. Jesus himself is the payment for our sin (Romans 3:25). Jesus has also defeated the powers of spiritual oppression and has rescued us into His kingdom (Colossians 1:13). For those stuck in the Self-help quadrant, Jesus alone is the way, or GPS, providing the path forward. Jesus alone makes us useful for the kingdom when we surrender our lives to Him as our Savior and Lord.

Growing up in the Cascade foothills in the Pacific Northwest, hiking and camping were also favorite pastimes. From my youth to this day, the number one rule of enjoying the wilderness is to leave it in better condition than when you arrived. For some, leaving it better isn't

only a wilderness rule but a way of life. They even view
the Christian religion as being all about doing good works.
Using some form of supernatural math, they figure that if a
God exists, then a greater amount of good works might get
them into heaven when they die. Or, if their worldview is
vacant of God or an afterlife, at least leave the world better
off than when you arrived. Such people may be stuck in the
"I have the Answers" quadrant of the Calling and Caring
framework. Helping people connect their calling and caring
is vital since Jesus is alive and active today. Some might
easily accept that Jesus was a good teacher who did good
to others. Such people may even applaud Jesus since he
cared about the same things and people they care about.
However, the same people may stumble when confronted
that Jesus is still doing good to others through His followers
because Jesus is alive and active today. Those stuck in the "I
have the Answers" quadrant need to come to faith in Jesus
and may best hear the gospel from a co-laborer who brings
the love of Jesus as they are helping others in need.

There is an undercurrent in the United States as
people who have grown up in Evangelical Christian
churches are deconstructing their faith [13], leaving
the church, and many choosing not to identify with
Christianity or Jesus [14]. Some of these, commonly known
as exvangelicals[15,] grew up in the salvation culture of the
"Jesus is my Answer" quadrant. A hallmark of the "Jesus
is my Answer" quadrant is that we can't solve the world's
problems but can save souls. The Evangelical purity culture
spread through Evangelical churches partly fueled by a
belief that the primary goal of the gospel is populating
eternity and saving people from the troubles and trials

of this world. In some churches, purity became equal to salvation. Any stray thought was seen as a sin, and many teens with normal teen hormones caught up in the purity culture questioned the viability of their salvation[16]. The "Jesus is my Answer" quadrant is marked by high morality and a desire to keep cloistered and safe from the world. Yet, knowing Jesus and embracing the great commandment to love God must include the second half—loving others.

> Whatever happened to the two clarion calls of Jesus through both the Great Commandment and the Great Commission? Did Jesus give us a choice to select one over the other or to dismiss them both altogether? Certainly not! Like two wheels on a bicycle, both the Great Commandment and the Great Commission integrally link to move the individual believer and the church further as a Christ-centered witness in and to the world under the auspices of God's overarching mission. To fulfill Christ's mission, his followers must receive divine love in order to enact the Great Commandment and be empowered by the Holy Spirit to engage in the Great Commission. Following Christ as the perfect imago Dei, we too are to grow increasingly into the image of Jesus, becoming like Christ in word and deed to advance the Missio Dei through the Great Commission. (Chandler, 2017, pp 163-164)[17].

As church leaders, we must embrace our goal to release people mobilized daily on God's mission with Him. To be mobilized is to be sent; sent out into a messy world that does not value what God values or celebrate what God celebrates. We are sent out not to become like them but as ambassadors proclaiming in word and deed, "Be reconciled to God" (2 Corinthians 5:20).

Sending Posture

We need to correct our calling form so that we have sending posture. Everything we do needs to feed the goal of seeing each follower of Jesus in our care engaged in Jesus' mission, daily serving others through God's unique calling. (Ephesians 2:10,4:10-11; 1 Corinthians 7:17, 1 Peter 4:10-11). A 2022 Lifeway Research study found that 46% of Christians shared a Bible verse or story with a non-Christian loved one in the past six months. However, 78% of churchgoers said they had never shared how to become a Christian with someone[18].

Like my nagging Tennis Elbow from cycling with an improperly fitted bicycle, the church, and subsequently, the world, suffers because of our poor calling form and sending posture. God's mission of reconciling the world to Himself by employing Jesus' Church as ambassadors (2 Corinthians 5:16-21) is not optional. Embracing sending posture and engaging daily in God's mission is critical. As church leaders, we must lead by example, engaging daily in God's mission. Each day, we are invited to ask God, "What is my role in Your mission today?" Because we are called to lead, it is our responsibility to help others to connect with God and His mission, to be equipped with their identity in

Christ and their calling, and to be released to engage daily in God's mission.

The next chapter will examine how we begin correcting our form and gaining sending posture. We will begin by looking at ourselves as leaders and then how we might encourage others to live sent.

CHAPTER 6 -END NOTES

1. Terkel, S. (2011). *Working: People Talk About What They Do All Day and How They Feel About What They Do*. The New Press.

2. *Definition of AMBITION*. (2024, October 22). https://www.merriam-webster.com/dictionary/ambition

3. Maslow, A. H. (1981). *Motivation and personality*. Prabhat Prakashan.

4. Sherman, A. L. (2011). *Kingdom Calling: Vocational Stewardship for the Common Good*. InterVarsity Press.

5. Frankl, V. E. (1992). *Man's search for meaning: An introduction to logotherapy, 4th ed* (I. Lasch, Trans.; p. 196). Beacon Press.

6. Eldredge, B. (2023). *The Paradise King: The Tragic History and Spectacular Future of Everything According to Jesus of Nazareth*. Blaine Eldredge.

7. Jethani, S. (2011). *With: Reimagining the Way You Relate to God* (First Edition). Thomas Nelson.

8. McGee, R. (2003). *The Search For Significance: Seeing Your True Worth Through God's Eyes* (Revised ed. edition). Thomas Nelson.

9. Dave Ramsey [@DaveRamsey]. (2024, March 5). *78% of Americans are living paycheck to paycheck. Basically, that means almost 8 out of 10 people probably can't afford the home they're living in and the car they're driving. They might not even have the cash to cover the next emergency that pops*

up. Your income is your most https://t.co/TzQfk8awK8 [Tweet]. Twitter. https://x.com/DaveRamsey/status/1765094292450599260

10. Carmelitequotes. (2021, February 12). Quote of the day, 12 February: Brother Lawrence. *Carmelite Quotes*. https://carmelitequotes. blog/2021/02/11/brolawrence-ltr1-deathcomesonce/

11. Strecker, J. (2020). *Church effectiveness: Organizational culture, religiosity, sense of community and civic engagement* [Dissertation].

12. Idleman, K. (2016). *Not a Fan Updated and Expanded: Becoming a Completely Committed Follower of Jesus* (Updated, Expanded ed. edition). Zondervan.

13. Caputo, J. D. (2007). *What would Jesus deconstruct? (The church and postmodern culture): the good news of postmodernism for the church*. Baker Academic.

14. Burge, R. P. (2021). *The nones: Where they came from, who they are, and where they are going*. Fortress Press.

15. McCammon, S. (2024). *The Exvangelicals: Loving, Living, and Leaving the White Evangelical Church*. St. Martin's Press.

16. Boesch, S. (2021). *My Church Told Me I Needed Sex Addicts Anonymous. Here's What Happened When I Went*. HUFFPOST Personal. https://www. huffpost.com/entry/sex-addiction-evangelicals-religion_n_60b237f0e4b 04ddf13ee60fb

17. Chandler, D. (2017). Godly love: The primary missional virtue. In N. A. Finn & K. S. Whitfield (Eds.), *Spirituality for the Sent: Casting a New Vision for the Missional Church* (pp. 162–182). IVP Academic.

18. Leake, M. (2024, July 22). *How Pastors Can Encourage Others to Consider Vocational Ministry*. Lifeway Research. https://research.lifeway.com/2024/07/22/how-pastors-can-encourage-others-to-consider-vocational-ministry/

CHAPTER 7

STARTING CHANGE

Haven't I commanded you: be strong and
courageous? Do not be afraid or discouraged, for
the Lord your God is with you wherever you go."
Joshua 1:9

The greatest cause of atheism in the world today is
Christians who acknowledge Jesus with their lips
and walk out the door and deny Him by their lives.
Brennan Manning

Change Starts With You

Our churches will not revive if there is no change. So, where
does change begin in our churches? If you're reading this,
you are probably a church leader—a pastor, elder, deacon,
trustee, director, volunteer youth worker, Bible study
leader, or another ministry leader. So, I know you probably
don't want to hear this, but by reading this book, change is
already starting because it is starting with you. You might
ask why I don't want to hear that. I want to change. But do
you? Change begins with you changing. Change doesn't

begin with your plans, methods, materials, processes, or people. Change begins with you.

Furthermore, leading change is not much fun at first because change will only begin when you start doing things differently than you've done in the past. That means doing things differently on Sunday morning but, more importantly, doing things differently Monday through Saturday. Change isn't easy. Change isn't popular. Yet, change is essential for you, the people you lead, and for your church to flourish.

Pastor and sociologist Ryan Berg joined the Rainer leadership group for a podcast in May 2024 to discuss how many churches exist in the United States[1]. Berg reported that the number of churches in the United States ranged between 350,000 and 400,000 churches. Berg noted that there is about one church per every 1000 people in the United States. How large is your church? The average church in the United States is about 100 people. Based on Berg's numbers, each average church does not reach about 900 people.

What does counting the number of churches in the United States have to do with change beginning in my church? Change in your church begins when you prioritize engaging in God's mission. In 2 Corinthians 5:19, Paul reminds us that God's mission is reconciling people back to himself through Christ Jesus. Jesus gives the same mission to every church in Matthew 28:16- 20. Change will begin in your church when you prioritize sharing your faith in Jesus with others, Monday through Saturday. If church leaders everywhere prioritized sharing their faith with others throughout the week and if, in one year, each church leader saw only one person begin to follow Jesus, the church in the United States would grow by almost half a million people per year. Imagine the impact if all the leaders in every church were willing to embrace change and live differently.

Making the Change

As followers of Jesus, we all know that we are supposed to share our faith in Jesus with others. Weekly sermons, Bible studies, conferences, and devotionals regularly challenge us to evangelize. Evangelism is an uncommon word in our culture. We only talk about evangelism when we talk about sharing our faith in Jesus with others. However, the word evangelism is rich in meaning and might hold the key to empowering us to share our faith in Jesus with others, or what I will call *personal evangelism*. Personal evangelism is about you personally introducing others to Jesus. Personal evangelism is different than group evangelism, and it's different than preaching a sermon, teaching a class, leading a bible study, writing a blog, or making a social media post. Personal evangelism is where change starts. As leaders of Jesus' movement, the church, you must prioritize sharing your faith in Jesus with others you encounter daily. How does the word "evangelism" connect with "sharing our faith in Jesus" with others? And why do we find personal evangelism so difficult? Growing in our understanding of personal evangelism can be a source of empowerment and inspiration for us all.

Before we dig into the word evangelism and paint a picture of what it looks like to share our faith in Jesus, we need to address barriers to personal evangelism. Most of Jesus' followers will encounter three main barriers when introducing others to Jesus: fear, lack of knowledge, and lack of opportunity. I like to call these barriers because a barrier is something, often temporary and movable, that keeps us from going somewhere or doing something. The word 'barrier' also works better in our headspace. It is easy for us to feel guilty when someone challenges us to engage in personal evangelism. We often feel like we are not doing enough when we hear how few people follow Jesus in our communities. Feeling guilty or insufficient will not motivate us to introduce people to Jesus. Likewise, making those we lead feel guilty will not motivate them to share Jesus with others. Yet, barriers are things we can overcome. Overcoming the barriers of fear, lack of knowledge, and lack of opportunity might help us and others join God daily on His mission.

The Barrier of Fear

When it comes to personal evangelism, many of us often find ourselves behind a barrier that feels like an unclimbable wall. The wall before us is familiar and has a foundation firmly planted in our fear of being accepted or liked. The barrier of fear is rooted in our need to be loved and is common to all humans—even extroverts. Overcoming the barrier of fear is significant because it is all about relationships. As humans, God wired us for relationships. We find our need to be in relationships with others in Genesis 2:18, as God declares it is not good for humans to be alone. The scientific disciplines of psychology and sociology have benefitted from work on Attachment Theory by John Bowlby[2]. Attachment Theory affirms what we find in Genesis chapter two. Humans need to be in relationships with other humans to survive. Our fear that others might dislike us is part of being human. Yet the key to overcoming the barrier of fear lies in the root of our fear—love.

While the scientific worldview will point toward evolution and say humans need relationships with other humans to survive, a biblical worldview recognizes God as the creator and the source of love.

> Dear friends, let us love one another, because love is from God, and everyone who loves has been born of God and knows God. The one who does not love does not know God, because God is love. God's love was revealed among us in this way: God sent his one and only Son into the world so that we might live through him. Love consists in this: not that we loved God, but that he loved us and sent his Son to be the atoning sacrifice for our sins. Dear friends, if God loved us in this way, we also must love one another (1 John 4:7-11, CSB).

John is writing these words to those already following Jesus. A little later, in verse 18 of the same chapter, John teaches that love conquers fear. But what about our love for those who are not following Jesus? Well, John is indeed writing to the church. Still, a biblical picture of God's love urges us to reflect on the fact that God loves all the people he created (John 3:16). When we focus on our love for others and allow our love for others to grow greater than our fear of being rejected, love can overcome the barrier of fear keeping us from introducing others to Jesus. Only love will conquer fear. Change in you and your church begins by learning to love outsiders enough to introduce them to Jesus.

Lack of Knowledge

The second barrier we encounter when introducing others to Jesus is a lack of knowledge. Too often, we feel that we don't know enough about Jesus to tell outsiders His good news. It's possible that the barrier of lack of knowledge isn't a big problem for leaders within the church. However, the barrier of lack of knowledge can impact us in two ways. The first way is obvious—we don't know how to introduce others to Jesus. Here we lack the knowledge, training, and disciplemaking to be a good witness for Jesus. The second way that the barrier of lack of knowledge can impact us is less obvious—we feel that to share our faith in Jesus, we need to share the entire gospel and a complete plan of salvation. In other words, the barrier of a lack of knowledge can impact us because either we don't know the gospel (the good news of Jesus) well enough or because of time or other issues, we feel we can't or won't be able to share enough of a plan of salvation to introduce others to Jesus properly.

A lack of knowledge might seem easier to overcome than the barrier of fear. Solid Christian teachers have developed sermon series, curriculum, bible studies, training videos, and other tools over the last 50 years to help train people to share a simple plan of salvation and their faith in Jesus Christ with others. Whether you're pulling out a little booklet, drawing a diagram on the back of a napkin, or using a five-letter pneumonic device, there are many methods that we can use to tell the good news of Jesus to those who've never heard God's story. Yet, the tools we use to teach people how to share the good news of Jesus might reinforce the barrier of lack of knowledge.

Not long after I began following Jesus, I learned to tell others about my faith in Jesus. I was handed the little booklet and challenged to memorize the it word for word. The purpose of memorizing the booklet was to recite it while the person I was talking to had the chance to read it themselves. The first time I shared the gospel booklet with someone, I was overwhelmed by the fear that I didn't know the contents well enough; the barrier of lack of knowledge blocked me. Once I had memorized the booklet, I went off to the streets of Seattle to ask people if I could share the good news of Jesus with them using my little booklet. Surprisingly, people are busy. Especially people you don't know. Sometimes, as I began sharing the gospel, suddenly, there was an uneasy shuffle, darting glances, or a quick peek at a watch, and my listeners would revoke the invitation to share. With a claim of busyness, the strangers would be off, leaving with an incomplete gospel presentation. There was no opportunity to ask questions and no chance for follow-up the next day. I held a somewhat empty reassurance that I may have planted a seed. The barrier of lack of knowledge, not knowing enough to share the good news of Jesus, and not being able to share the entire gospel message is rooted in how we understand the gospel.

In his book *How God Became King*[3], NT Wright
suggests that we must clarify what we mean when we use
the word gospel. Wright points out that the first four books
of the New Testament are each called gospels. However,
when we share the good news of Jesus, we don't share all
89 chapters found in the four gospel accounts. We don't
even focus on one gospel account; we blend Mathew's
28 chapters, Mark's 16 chapters, Luke's 24 chapters, and
John's 21 chapters into one cohesive story. Why? Because
that's what the apostles and Paul did when we see them
sharing the gospel in the book of Acts. There are seven, or
some would argue, eight times in the book of Acts when the
gospel is shared[4].

Each time, what is shared is a little different. That's not to
say that every sharing of the gospel story didn't contain
the essentials of the gospel message. Essentials such as the
gospel is God's story, and Jesus is the one God sent with
authority to be Lord, savior, and Judge. That Jesus was
crucified, resurrected, and ascended. People are separated
from God by their rebellion and sins and unable to save
themselves. God calls people to faith in Jesus, demonstrated
by repentance- turning away from sin and toward God.
These gospel essentials are a little different than the book I
first memorized. Yet, the important parts of the gospel were
in that booklet, including that God is God, Jesus is God's
son, and the sacrifice for sins. Jesus died and rose again,
and I needed to repent of my sins and have faith in Jesus.
But the booklet I first memorized, the gospel summary I
learned, was based on the consequences of my continued
disbelief. The booklet was a plan of salvation with a gospel
essentially reduced to focus on salvation or how to avoid

hell and get to heaven. It is not surprising that much of my early faith was concerned with avoiding hell rather than walking with Jesus.

Reading through the book of Acts, I see that the early church didn't declare any consequences as they presented the good news of Jesus. The apostles focused on Jesus as the way to reconnect with God, the source of life and shalom. As a result, the early church didn't struggle with not knowing the entire gospel or not being able to share the complete salvation plan.

If Matthew, Mark, Luke, and John are each an account of the gospel of Jesus, the seven or eight gospel sermons of Paul and the apostles in the book of Acts are the gospel of Jesus, and if the little booklet I memorized, when I began following Jesus, is the gospel—and they are not all the same—then what is the gospel? The gospel of Jesus Christ is not easy to define. Pastors, teachers, scholars, and authors have written numerous books to answer the question: what is the gospel? Defining the gospel has sparked arguments, split denominations, and strained friendships. Scott McKnight offers a great resource discussing the gospel's content and historically chronicling the gospel's journey from Jesus' day to today. I recommend reading through Scott McKnight's *The King Jesus Gospel*[4]. Whether or not you agree with McKnight's conclusions, after reading the *King Jesus Gospel*, you will have entered a thorough discussion, which will hopefully help you define what you mean when you use the term gospel.

The goal of this chapter is not to determine the perfect definition of the gospel but rather to overcome the barrier of lack of knowledge so that we can change and our churches can change. Therefore, we will adopt McKnight's definition of the gospel found in The King Jesus Gospel for our discussion. The gospel is Jesus' story as the fulfillment of Israel's story as the fulfillment of God's redemptive story.

Viewing the gospel as Jesus' story, as the fulfillment of Israel's story, as the fulfillment of God's redemptive story puts a kink in overcoming the barrier of lack of knowledge. With such a robust gospel definition, it would seem that none of us, or at least very few followers of Jesus, have enough knowledge to convey the gospel to someone who does not know God's story. However, as we study the four main accounts of Jesus' story in the New Testament, along with the expressions of the gospel in the book of Acts, we see that Paul and the apostles never shared Jesus' entire story. Sometimes, they didn't even share enough of the gospel for someone to decide. Other times, people surrender their lives to Jesus after hearing little of Jesus' story. We see anecdotally that sharing and knowing the whole story of Jesus is not essential for someone to come to faith in Christ. Therefore, we need to dig deeper if we're going to overcome the barrier of lack of knowledge.

We usually use evangelism when talking about telling others of Jesus' story. Evangelism is an English term derived from the Greek word euangelion, which translates as 'gospel'. In the 1st century Greek-speaking world, euangelion or gospel summoned the image of good news or good tidings[5]. There is a tablet created a few years before the birth of Jesus in Priene, modern-day Turkey, about the birth of Caesar Augustus. The people of Priene declare that time centered around the birth of emperor Augustus. The tablet declares that the birth of emperor Augustus is the euangelion or the beginning of 'good tidings' or 'good news'. The use of euangelion before the coming of Jesus demonstrates that people used the word euangelion in political discourse. It's possible that 30 years before Jesus's birth, when Pompey captured Jerusalem, Rome sent out messengers to proclaim the good news of Rome's rule over Israel. These messengers would have been called evangelists[6].

Evangelists or tellers of good news are not uncommon in our world today. Indeed, the news media often reports stories of bad news. However, the tellers of good news in Western culture are not attached to institutions or organizations. Social media posts about the birth of a child, a significant life achievement, a community fundraiser, a special event, or even the opening of a new restaurant are all declarations of good news. Many people we work with who struggle with barriers to sharing Jesus' story practice being evangelists or proclaimers of good news in their personal lives.

Engaging in personal evangelism requires overcoming the barrier of lack of knowledge. The barrier of lack of knowledge crumbles when we realize that most of us will never grasp every detail of the gospel, Jesus' story as the fulfillment of Israel's story as the fulfillment of God's redemptive story. In Mark chapter five, we find the story of the Gadarene Demoniac. We never learned this man's name; we only know that he lives in the region of the Gadarenes, is demonized, and that either he or those who care for him have repeatedly attempted to restrain him, binding him with chains. Yet we learned this man is so strong nobody can restrain him. Beyond the man's natural strength, the Bible also assures us that he was demonized. Jesus addresses the demons, casting them out into a herd of pigs. The herd of pigs helps us understand that the region of the Gadarenes was in the area settled by gentile Romans. Therefore, the Gadarene demoniac was most likely a gentile who was clueless that God had a redemptive plan, that God had been revealing his redemptive plan through Israel. The Roman Gaderean may have also been unaware the man named Jesus had anything to do with God's story.

Jesus, seeing the man's plight, has compassion and commands the demons to leave him. The demons leave the man and demonize a herd of pigs, causing the pigs to rush down into the water and die. Mark tells us that when people heard what happened, they found Jesus and the Gadarene man, who was now fully clothed in his right mind. The whole encounter caused a serious monetary concern for the townspeople when they found their herd of about 2000 pigs destroyed. The gathering crowd demands Jesus to leave.

> As he was getting into the boat, the man who had been demon-possessed begged him earnestly that he might remain with him. Jesus did not let him but told him, "Go home to your own people, and report to them how much the Lord has done for you and how he has had mercy on you." So he went out and began to proclaim in the Decapolis how much Jesus had done for him, and they were all amazed (Mark 5:18-20, CSB).

It is generous to claim that the healed Gadarene man knew much of God's redemptive plan or Jesus. All this man knew was that Jesus healed him and set him free. Yes, he knew that Jesus called himself Lord. He also knew that Jesus was compassionate and merciful. The man also knew that he was no longer tormented; he had been set free. Jesus sent the man to tell others what little he knew, and the Gadarene man proclaimed the gospel of Jesus Christ.

The story of the Gadarene demoniac gives us hope for overcoming the barrier of lack of knowledge. Earlier, I mentioned that this barrier might result from how we view the gospel and talk and train about evangelism. The barrier of lack of knowledge may be the most difficult to overcome because we need to change how we think. The Gadarene man went out with no background and no training. Could he share the entire gospel? We don't know what he knew about God and His redemptive story. All the Gadarene man could do was share what he did know—Jesus healed him and set him free. Not only could the Gadarene man only share what he knew, and that seemed to be enough for Jesus, but he could only share as much as people were willing to listen. The same is true for you and me. We must change how we think about personal evangelism and sharing the gospel. We need to season our understanding of evangelism with the concept of gospeling. Gospeling points people toward Jesus as much as we can and as much as others allow, as often as possible. Instead of evangelizing or sharing a plan of salvation, what if we engaged in gospeling?

Gospeling

Gospeling is a term that I first heard from McKnight (who
may have picked it up from NT Wright). Gospeling refers
to everything we do that expresses a part or the whole of
the gospel. Gospeling is a proclamation of good news, so
gospeling is evangelism. Yet, unlike traditional models and
methods of evangelism and evangelism training, gospeling
does not leverage success based on sharing the entire
gospel. Sometimes, gospeling can occurs without words
through how we live our lives. George Müller and his work
with the Ashley Down orphanage comes to mind. George's
life of surrender to God's mission and his prayerful
dependence on God's provision resounds like a train horn
declaring that Jesus' victory on the cross is good news to
everyone[7]. Gospeling shines a light on Jesus through our
credibility, gospeling points others toward Jesus through
our actions, and gospeling declares the truth and presence
of Jesus through intentional conversations. Gospeling sums
up how we live as disciplemakers among those around
us. Gospeling is all about who we are, how we live, and
the words we use to intentionally reflect the love of Christ,
displaying God's justice and justness, pointing people
toward Jesus as the one true King.

Gospeling is what Jesus meant by 'go' in Matthew
28:19 and 20. You may have heard in a sermon that the
verb commands in this passage begins with the command
to go. I won't get into all the Greek here, but the sentence
structure in the Greek for 'go' makes it a command, but
it is a dependent command. Here is how it works, 'go' is
not like we understand what it means to go. Usually, 'to
go' means leaving someplace. An English understanding

and translation of "go" in Matthew 28:19 has been used to inspire and justify taking the gospel worldwide by sending missionaries—the result is the spread of the gospel by a few worldwide. However, in Matthew 28:19, the command "go" is dependent on the command to make disciples. Therefore, going and making disciples becomes one compound command. "Go," in Matthew 28:19, is a command to organize and order our lives so that we are intentionally living on mission, introducing people to Jesus and teaching them to follow Him—every day and everywhere we go. The Simple command of 'go' coupled with the command to make disciples is expressed in our lives as gospeling.

Gospeling requires us to change how we think about evangelism and sharing the gospel. Gospeling requires us to think about sharing our faith in Jesus not as an activity but as a value—the value of gospel intentionality. Valuing gospel intentionality drives us with a purpose, a mission, but not one of our own design, instead with God's kingdom mission.

Gospeling sums up the command to go in the great commission. Gospeling occurs in our worship and teaching at church. Gospeling can happen in our homes, at the grocery store, the coffee shop, restaurant, dry cleaners, and the gym. Gospeling takes place wherever we are as we go throughout our normal life. Gospeling is how we engage with God in his 2 Corinthians chapter 5, reconciling the world to Himself. Gospeling is how God makes His plea through us—God's plea, which the CSB translates as "come back to God."

Lack of Opportunity

Allowing our love to grow for those whom God loves will help us overcome the barrier of fear. And gospeling helps us overcome the barrier of lack of knowledge. However, gospeling reveals most Christ followers' biggest barrier regarding personal evangelism. The third barrier is a lack of opportunity. Personal evangelism is a struggle for many simply because they do not know anyone who hasn't heard about Jesus.

There is little research on how many Christians do not interact with non-Christians in the United States or around the world. However, there is research on how many non-Christians personally know a Christian. According to Lifeway research, over 80% of those belonging to a non-Christian or no religion do not have a personal relationship with a Christian[8]. In the United States, the Pew Research Center notes that one in three adults considers themselves ranked among the religious 'nones,' and 20% of adults do not have a personal relationship with a Christ follower[9]. Many Christians do not have relationships with non-Christians. Between Sunday morning services, midweek small groups, and volunteering in church or community ministries, many Christians have little time for outsiders to God's family. We share our lives with those who are already learning to follow Jesus.

Hebrews chapter 10 addresses a problem where Christ's followers in the early church were not spending enough time together. The author of Hebrews reminds us not to give up meeting together: "not neglecting to gather together, as some are in the habit of doing, but encouraging each other, and all the more as you see the

day approaching" (Hebrews 10:25, CSB). It is difficult to
believe, in our post-pandemic culture, that the same people
in churches who fought local governments to be allowed
to meet during COVID-19 lockdowns would need much
encouragement to meet together. Even though current
research identifies a regular church attendee as someone
going to church once per month, the problem pendulum
has swung to the other extreme over the centuries. Now,
we need to encourage Christ's followers to overcome the
barrier of lack of opportunity, get out of their Christian
cloistered clusters, and get to know some non-Christians,
some outsiders to the family of God.

    I get it. There's only so much time in the day.
Paul discusses the difficulty of spending too much time
with outsiders to God's family. In 2 Corinthians 6:15,
Paul asks, "What does a believer have in common with
an unbeliever?" While Paul asks a valid question, Jesus
modeled the habit of eating meals and socializing with
people God loved even though they were rebels, sinners,
enemies of God, and outsiders to God's family. The gospel
writers did a great job of capturing Jesus living on God's
mission. Jesus crossed borders and boundaries to build
friendships with people who were outsiders to God's
family[10]. Today, crossing borders to invite people usually
looks like international missions. However, crossing
boundaries may be less familiar. We cross boundaries when
we intentionally step out of our comfort zones to serve
and uplift people different from us. Like borders, we cross
boundaries to invite outsiders to become insiders in God's
family. And guess what? When Jesus crossed borders and
boundaries, it made some of his peers uncomfortable, and

when we cross borders and boundaries, be prepared; we might make people uncomfortable, too.

Overcoming the barrier of lack of opportunity requires us to cross borders and boundaries. Through the history of the Church's global missions efforts, it is easy to understand what we mean by crossing borders. Crossing borders might involve visiting another country or a different language group on a short-term or long-term mission trip. But we can cross borders in our own communities. Crossing borders might mean building relationships with people whose primary language or culture differs from your own. Crossing boundaries differs from crossing borders. Crossing boundaries involves building friendships with people who might have a different peer group. Yes, friendships. Crossing boundaries is messy and requires an investment of time. They may live in a different part of town or have a different economic class, social class, or ethnicity. Crossing boundaries involves building friendships with people with values or goals different from yours. It is possible that crossing boundaries means building a friendship with someone who likes a different hobby or roots for a different sports team than you do.

If we plan to overcome the barrier of lack of opportunity, we will need to cross borders and boundaries. When we cross borders and boundaries, we might upset some people. We must not forget that God's mission for us and the purpose of personal evangelism is to proclaim the good news of Jesus and invite people to be part of God's family. We may upset people, not by how we act, but because we live for and proclaim that Jesus is King.

"If the world hates you, understand that it hated me before it hated you. If you were of the world, the world would love you as its own. However, because you are not of the world, but I have chosen you out of it, the world hates you. Remember the word I spoke to you: 'A servant is not greater than his master.' If they persecuted me, they will also persecute you. If they kept my word, they will also keep yours. But they will do all these things to you on account of my name, because they don't know the one who sent me (John 15:18-21, CSB).

The solution to overcoming a lack of opportunity is getting to know people outside God's family. Please note that persecution, people outside of God's family becoming upset when we proclaim Jesus, is not a barrier to engaging in personal evangelism. If we intentionally live on God's mission as he redeems and restores us to Himself through Jesus Christ, we will upset some people. Overcoming the barrier of lack of opportunity requires us to cross borders and boundaries and build friendships with outsiders to God's family. Overcoming the barrier of lack of opportunity is a call to intentionally live with God on His mission.

Many of Jesus' followers lack opportunity simply because we do not intentionally apply God's mission to our daily lives. What are the rhythms of your day, week, and year? What do you intentionally do to make friends with outsiders to the family of God? Working adults might find people on the job who don't know Jesus. The

inclusivity movements in Western culture have most
employers weary of spiritual expressions and conversations
on the job. In the United States, Title VII mandates that
employers allow for religious expression on the job—to a
point[11]. Religious expression cannot impose hardship on
the employer or be viewed as harassing other employees[12].
Personal evangelism during work hours can be a headache
for employers and human resource managers. So, if work
is your primary place to meet outsiders to God's family,
how are you connecting with outsiders after work? What
do you need to do to change the rhythm of your life to
cross borders and boundaries, building friendships with
outsiders to God's family?

Are you in a season with kids in school? How are
you engaging with other parents? Do you attend sports,
music, theater, speech and debate, or other activities
seeking to connect with those outside the family of God?
Don't overlook the significance of being on campus and
engaging in middle and high school ministry. Young
people who don't know Jesus flood the halls of your
local public schools. Even after the COVID-19 pandemic
restrictions have faded, public schools are still hubs where
different groups of people come together with nothing in
common other than their kids' age. How are you reaching
the students in your community? You may not have time
to volunteer, coach, substitute teach, or mentor a young
person, and that's OK. Teenagers can be difficult to relate
to and reach. Focus on meeting their parents, and then how
might you support and train those reaching the students in
your community with the good news of Jesus?

What is your reputation in your community? Are you out in your community enough for those outside the family of God to get to know you? Do you live in a way guided and guarded by your family-of-God values? Do you have a reputation for not judging those whose way of life differs from yours? Does your reputation declare what you are for rather than what you are against?

> "You are the salt of the earth. But if the salt should lose its taste, how can it be made salty? It's no longer good for anything but to be thrown out and trampled under people's feet. "You are the light of the world. A city situated on a hill cannot be hidden. No one lights a lamp and puts it under a basket, but rather on a lampstand, and it gives light for all who are in the house. In the same way, let your light shine before others, so that they may see your good works and give glory to your Father in heaven (Matthew 5:13-16).

The gospel of Jesus Christ only makes sense when we understand that the gospel is good news for the entire world. Jesus is God's provision for the entire world. Jesus's victory on the cross brings about the beginning of his kingdom, which means there is a different ruler in charge than what the principalities and powers of this world would have us believe. Jesus fulfilled everything in Israel's story, which is God's redemptive story, and amid his death on the cross, Jesus won a victory over sin, death, and the powers of darkness. Jesus' victory is good news. Jesus' victory brings about our salvation, gives us new life, brings us into the family of God, makes us the temple of God, and initiates a new order—an order in which Jesus' people living Jesus' way bring life even in a world influenced by enemy powers and principalities who remain steeped in sin and death. Jesus is King. Do others see you live differently because Jesus is your King?

The Changing You

If you are a leader in a church, much of this chapter has been review. Yet, if you are like me, it is needed review. Again and again, I need to be reminded that I have been saved for a purpose—God's purpose. We all need to engage in smaller communities that practice missional accountability. God has given me a mission—to make disciples. God has also given me a role to help lead and restore the movement of the Church. As leaders in the movement of the church, change begins with us. We must be willing to change. We must never let go of what is important, the foundations of our faith. Yet, we must be willing to change the way we live. To allow the Holy Spirit and the Word of God to realign us to God's mission (2 Timothy 3:16). We must also be willing to be the living example to the people we lead (Romans 12:2) as we help them surrender to God, hold on to the foundation of their faith, and change the way they live to realign to God's redemptive mission. Change starts with you and begins when you prioritize personal evangelism.

CHAPTER 7 – END NOTES

1. *The Burge Report: Are There Too Many Churches in the United States?* (n.d.). Church Answers. Retrieved July 1, 2024, from https:// churchanswers.com/podcasts/rainer-on-leadership/the-burge-report-are-there-too-many-churches-in-the-united-states/

2. Bowlby, J. (1979). The Bowlby-Ainsworth attachment theory. *Behavioral and Brain Sciences*, 2(4), 637–638. https://doi.org/10.1017/S0140525X00064955

3. Wright, N. T. (2016). *How God became king: The forgotten story of the gospels* (Reprint edition). HarperOne.

4. McKnight, S., & Willard, N. T. W. and D. (2016). *The King Jesus Gospel: The Original Good News Revisited* (Revised edition). Zondervan.

5. Murphy, C. (2020). *The Priene Calendar Inscription.* Departmet of Religious Studies, Santa Clara University. https://webpages.scu.edu/ftp/cmurphy/courses/sctr027/artifacts/priene-calendar.htm

6. Cady, N. (2019, January 9). The Gospel of Caesar Augustus, & What It Tells Us About the Gospel of Jesus Christ. *Theology for the People.* https://nickcady.org/2019/01/09/the-gospel-of-caesar-augustus-what-it-tells-us-about-the-gospel-of-jesus-christ/

6. *George Mueller—Inspiring Life and Legacy.* (n.d.). Christianity.Com. Retrieved July 3, 2024, from https://www.christianity.com/church/

church-history/church-history-for-kids/george-mueller-orphanages-built-by-prayer-11634869.html

8. Earls, A. (2021, June 9). *The Places Where No One Knows a Christian.* Lifeway Research. https://research.lifeway.com/2021/06/09/the-places-where-no-one-knows-a-christian/

9. Alper, G. A. S., Patricia Tevington, Justin Nortey, Michael Rotolo, Asta Kallo and Becka A. (2024, January 24). Religious 'Nones' in America: Who They Are and What They Believe. *Pew Research Center.* https://www.pewresearch.org/religion/2024/01/24/religious-nones-in-america-who-they-are-and-what-they-believe/

10. Bosch, D. J. (2011). *Transforming mission: Paradigm shifts in theology of mission.* Orbis Books.
D'Agostino, T. (2023, April 27). *Religious expression at work: Where should you draw the line?* https://www.hrmorning.com/articles/religious-expression-at-work-draw-the-line/

11. *Title VII of the Civil Rights Act of 1964.* (n.d.). US EEOC. Retrieved July 8, 2024, from https://www.eeoc.gov/statutes/title-vii-civil-rights-act-1964

CHAPTER 8

REVIVE – THE OVERVIEW

From the Issacharites, who understood the times
and knew what Israel should do: 200 chiefs with all
their relatives under their command.
1 Chronicles 12:32a

"We believe the church's purpose is to glorify
God, not to make people happy. The church does
not exist for believers or unbelievers; it exists for
God's glory, for the equipping of believers, and the
church is God's missionary in the world."
Ed Stetzer

The box is empty, and the plastic bags have all been
opened. Early in his Lego building hobby, I tried to teach
my son to patiently sort each Lego brick before beginning
to build. This chapter is a nod to my son and a nod to Peter
Greig. When I picked up my first book on prayer by Peter
Greig, I was astonished to find the first section of his book
offered an overview of everything else. Grieg boasted that
the entire book could be read in just a few minutes by

reading one chapter. My son does the same thing with Lego sets. Instead of looking at the manuals, he often tries to build his latest set by only looking at the picture on the box. Greig's overview indeed gives a good understanding of the content of the book, yet you miss how different things are connected and the thoughts and stories that support the ideas. Likewise, the picture on the Lego box describes the outside of the finished model well, but my son's approach often overlooks hidden parts, new building techniques, and the creative investment of the set's designers. As you read through this chapter, you will get the gist of this book in about ten minutes. You will find the following composed thought by thought rather than chapter by chapter.

The following sections will take you through the broad brushstrokes of the book. As a last chapter, we will focus mainly with the "why" and "what's next." You will need to dive into the individual chapters to discover how everything connects. I am intentionally limiting the content of each section to what I might share with you if we were to run into one another in an elevator. Therefore, if you have read the previous chapters first, this last chapter will galvanize the entire book for you. But, if you are starting with this chapter, please let me give you my elevator speech. Hopefully, after the elevator speech, you might feel encouraged to grab a cup of coffee and sit with me as we share ideas and mutually revitalize one another's fire for God's mission and His movement, which we call the Church.

The Watchers on the Wall

"But the godly will flourish like palm trees and grow strong like the cedars of Lebanon...Even in old age they will still produce fruit; they will remain vital and green" (Psalm 92:12 &14, NLT). The church is blessed at this time in history to consist of many different generations. While few remain in our ranks from the greatest generation, you are likely to find Traditionalists, Boomers, X'ers, Millennials, Gen Z, and Gen Alpha on a Sunday morning. For those of us in the upper half of the generations, our fruit-producing years may seem limited according to the world's standards. But not so with God! Even though on our watch, we have seen a decline in church attendance and biblical literacy, an increase of those claiming no religious affiliation, and a cultural sub-current of exvangelicals and those deconstructing their faith. With God, we are not without hope.

The fruit produced by the older generations can no longer be measured in our accomplishments: the number of buildings we have built, the number of seats filled, the size of our budgets, or even the number of baptisms. The metrics of the past measure ministry activities and outcomes. The church is a movement, and movements multiply. The church is a multiplying movement, and those called to lead the movement of the church are called to mobilize people into the harvest field (Matthew 9:37-38) and to invest in others who will do the same (2 Timothy 2:2).

In Isaiah 62, the prophet Isaiah prays for the people of Jerusalem to have hope and to lean into the promise of God (Isaiah 62:6-7). While this prophecy was not meant as a

prescription for modern-day, the watchers on the wall were
called to pray day and night. These watchers were also
posted to remind the people of God's promises and that
God keeps His promises. These prayer-warrior-watchers
are commanded in verse 7 to "Give the Lord no rest until
he completes his work." Isaiah's watchers of the wall were
also watchers of the mission, God's mission. There is hope
on our watch as we mobilize the church, multiply ourselves
into the lives of others, and maintain an unwavering
commitment to God's mission. Let us remain atop the
walls, praying day and night until the throne room is filled
and overflowing with people representing every nation,
every tribe, and every tongue.

The Church is a Stuck Movement

Half a century ago mass evangelism crusades would
mobilize communities. People from various denominations
would band together, train together, pray together, and
invite others, filling stadiums. Thousands would surrender
to Jesus whether they were in person or watching the
live broadcast of the event at home on TV. Young men
and women working with parachurch ministries-built
relationships with teenagers, sharing the good news of
Jesus with students on public school campuses, colleges,
and universities. Volunteer youth workers offering nothing
but their time and free pizza might attract hundreds of
students to church buildings each week. We have seen the
movement of the church in action in our lifetime. Yet, today
the church seems stuck.

A prevailing theological and academic view of the
church supported by the late Timothy Keller[1], holds that

the Christian church has a dual nature—divine and human. The Christian church is both an invisible, supernatural, spiritual body and a visible, messy, entrenched in culture, organized gatherings of believers who interact with their community and culture. Socio-theology is an interdisciplinary approach to exploring how and why the church seems stuck. Sociology reflects the human nature of the church and theology the divine nature of the church. Socio-theology provides a new perspective reminding us of the identity of the church as the body of Christ and the calling of the Church to fulfill the great commandment and commission of God's mission.

Viewing the church through the lens of divine and human, socio-theology allows us to evaluate how and why the church is a stuck movement. As a movement the church is concerned with connecting with God and His mission, connecting people in community that encourages one another toward mobilization, and empowering and releasing people to live on mission. Connecting with God, connecting with others, and engaging in mission infused activity comprise the essential movement markers of the Christian church. The church might be a stuck movement because more emphasis has been placed on knowing about God and His mission than about engaging in missional activity with God in our families, schools, workplaces, community, and world.

Ecclesia-Motus

The Ecclesia-motus framework is an evidenced based framework developed through the interdisciplinary application of socio-theology using a social movement lens to understand people's engagement with their faith and church[2]. The Ecclesia-motus framework provides three domains for a new set of measures for the church— connection with God and His mission, connection with others, and living sent together. Each dimension in the framework is connected to the other two dimensions. Therefore, our connection with God grows as we connect with others and engage in God's mission. The new measures derived from the Ecclesia-motus framework provides the opportunity to infuse sending posture into a discipleship pathway or spiritual formation plan. The Ecclesia-motus framework is introduced in chapter three and then discussed in detail in chapter four. At first glance, the interconnectedness of the dimensions of the Ecclesia-motus framework may seem to be common sense. In many ways, it is common sense. Applying the Ecclesia-motus framework to a ministry may not require a complete overhaul. Rather, as we will see in chapter six, employing the Ecclesia-motus framework may make small yet significant adjustments that will increase the sending posture and movement mobilization of your church or ministry.

Here is a brief overview of the Ecclesia-motus framework. The first domain is connecting with God and His mission. The second domain of the framework is connecting with others in community of missional encouragement. It is in the second dimension of the framework where individuals are held accountable to practicing missional living. The third domain of the Ecclesia-motus frames work is living sent on God's mission with Him. The everyday engagement of Jesus' kingdom mission in the community, at work, at school, shopping, on a sports team, at a club meeting, or wherever your day takes you.

Shepherding Leadership

It is much easier to teach a group of people who show up in church on Sunday morning than to lead to lead countless individuals and groups engaging in messy spirit directed ministry to people who would never darken the door of a church. Unfortunately, the models of leadership gleaned from the marketplace do not reflect the challenges of leading the movement of the church. Shepherding Leadership is a leadership model derived from watching Jesus lead and elements of leadership as an art. Shepherding Leadership is a leadership model that focuses on the art of leading rather than the person as a leader. In Western culture, churches and ministries often rise and fall dependent on the leader. In 1 Corinthians chapter three, Paul chastises the Corinthian church for attaching themselves to human leaders rather than following Jesus together. Shepherding Leadership is needed to lead people in joining God on His mission. Shepherding Leadership leads people to focus and commit to God's mission as their purpose, protects people from being discouraged, distracted, or derailed, and serves people through a process which empowers and releases them on mission.

Shepherding Leaderships borrows three images from the shepherd metaphor. The shepherd's staff reflects how God guides us with love and grace as He leads us to connect our purpose with His mission, inviting us to join Him each day. The shepherd's rod reflects protection.

Shepherding Leadership protects people by helping
them remain connected and helping people avoid or
work through being discouraged, distracted, or derailed.
The shepherd's heart reflects leading with process. The
shepherd's heart drives us to lead with process, leveraging
our tools for spiritual formation or a discipleship pathway
to equip and empower people to flourish as disciplemakers
in their identity and to release them into their calling. It
may be affirming when people follow you, but it is beyond
this world exciting when you have a front row seat to see
God transform people as they join Him on His mission.

Sending posture – Calling and Caring

Every person and every church must find their role within
God's purpose. Why? Knowing and living your purpose
and role form the foundation for connecting your calling
with your caring—even if it changes over time. What is
God's purpose? How has God designed, impassioned, and
directed me in my role in His story, and where and when
can I live out my role? These are the three care questions
of a sending posture: why me, why here, why now? As
leaders we are both sent ones and senders of others. We
help people discover their purpose, their role, their calling.
We help our local church as an organization and the people
within answer the questions: Why me? Why here? Why
now? We actively practice sending posture as we help
people discover their calling, equipping, empowering, and
releasing them to live sent with God on His mission.

    If we are to help people discover their calling, we
will need to get to know them and what they care about.
The people we serve are mostly the products of their

histories. Their triumphs, failures, joys, and wounds. Personal histories mix with their personal experiences and opportunities informing what they care about. As we enter the stories of those we serve, we can lead people into a multiplying disciplemaking process.

We engage people in a disciplemaking process, helping them discover their identity in Christ, how God has fashioned them to care about people and problems, and how God invites them to engage in His kingdom mission. Leading through a disciplemaking process helps those we serve connect their calling with what they care about— God breaks their hearts for what breaks His heart. The disciplemaking process multiplies as God aligns their hearts with His , and they develop sending posture. Sending posture is practiced at the intersection of one's caring and God's kingdom calling as they are empowered and released to respond to God as He invites them to join Him on His mission.

Picture of Change

Most people seem like they do not like change. God never changes, and maybe it is human hubris that makes so many resistant to change. Yet, the one constant of the world we live in is change. The hard frost killed my tomato plants. A month earlier the tomato plants were thriving bushes producing fruit upon fruit. Months earlier the tomato plants were newly sprouted and seemed like they might not survive. Plants change, the seasons change, and we as humans change. Leaders lead people toward change, even if most people do not like change. Therefore, like it or not, leaders need to be willing to participate in the change they lead.

When we participate in the change we lead, we are not going first for others to follow. Going first works great when you are playing a kid's game walking through the woods. Instead, Shepherding Leadership challenges leaders to build the bridge we are walking on as we walk across it together with those we serve[3]. As we cross the bridge together with those we serve as leaders, we become a living picture of the mission as we follow God together[4]. As leaders we must be willing to humble ourselves and agree that we too need to change. What change do we need to make? We need to revive our fervor for personal evangelism.

Personal evangelism is about each of us, me and you, personally introducing others to Jesus. Personal evangelism is different than group evangelism, and it's different than preaching a sermon, teaching a class, leading a bible study, writing a blog, or making a social media post. Personal evangelism is where begins. As leaders in the movement of the church, we must prioritize sharing our faith in Jesus with others. Many of us encounter three main barriers to personal evangelism: the barrier of fear, the barrier of a lack of knowledge, and the barrier of a lack of opportunity. We overcome fear with love. We overcome a lack of opportunity through changing our rhythms to befriend outsiders to God's family. We overcome a lack of knowledge through gospeling. Gospeling is testifying that Jesus is Savior and King through our attitudes, action, and words. Gospeling elevates every interaction to an opportunity for personal evangelism. What does it mean to "share our faith in Jesus" with others? Growing in our understanding of personal evangelism can be a source of empowerment and inspiration for us all.

Who is Next?

If you are anything like me, you are probably reading this chapter first. Why not get the elevator pitch version of the book first? Yet, I hope you are willing to pause long enough to sit down for a cup of coffee and work through each chapter. In my small town, I have opportunity to choose from a variety of local artisan coffee roasters. Some are hobbyists, some are non-profits, and others curate coffee shop experiences. In our hurried culture, there is tremendous value in sitting with a thought long enough to process, to think, to agree, disagree, and integrate your thinking into your own life. So, if all you do is read this chapter, then please, pause and sit with the next few paragraphs for a little extra time. May God use them to revive His invitation to you to join Him on His mission.

Who is your next? Dr. Tim Weibe is the spiritual formation pastor at Brookside church in Omaha, Nebraska and author of *What Does It Mean to Follow Jesus?: A Clear, Biblical Picture of Discipleship* [5]. Dr. Weibe challenges people at all levels of leadership with this simple question: Who is your next? Who is the next person you are praying for, sharing Jesus with, training and equipping, mobilizing on mission, multiplying (preparing for movement leadership)? The simple question, "who is your next?", is at the starting line for your church to revive. I have no doubt that each of us desires to hear "well done" from Jesus one day (Matthew 25:21). But leaders in Jesus' kingdom need to be driven to ensure that those around us hear "well done" at the end of their time of serving. Not only do we need to ask ourselves the question of who is next, we need to train others to ask the question of themselves. Who is your next?

The great commission found in Matthew chapter 28 verses 18-20, at first glance, commands us to make disciples, connect them to God and His mission, and to train them in kingdom living. Yet, we need to view the entire passage together as a whole.

Jesus came near and said to them, "All authority has been given to me in heaven and on earth. Go, therefore, and make disciples of all nations, baptizing them in the name of the Father and of the Son and of the Holy Spirit, teaching them to observe everything I have commanded you. And remember, I am with you always, to the end of the age" (Matthew 28:18-20, CSB).

The command or process that Matthew is recoding in this passage goes beyond making individual disciples. Instead, Matthew is informing us that Jesus's command is to make disciplemakers or raise up disciplemakers. Matthew is describing the process Paul later used to train Timothy as a pattern for building churches. "What you have heard from me in the presence of many witnesses, commit to faithful men who will be able to teach others also" (2 Timothy 2:2, CSB). The intentionality of engaging, equipping, empowering, and releasing people to become disciplemakers that Matthew and Paul are describing does not present as a ministry model or a church growth process, but a movement. A disciplemaking movement.

As the coffee in your cup cools and our time comes to a close, there are a couple questions we need to ponder.

How committed to God's mission are you willing to be?
Is God's mission more important than the ways in which
you have or are currently experiencing church? Are you
secure in your identity in Christ? Do you know how your
calling and your caring intersect? Are you willing to release
others into their role in God's gospel mission? Can you
overcome the barriers to personal evangelism in your
own life? Will you embrace the church as a movement in
Jesus' kingdom even if it means your life will change? The
church must revive and embrace God's mission, becoming
the disciplemaking movement that transforms lives,
communities, and the world. Since, the church must revive,
and change begins with you, there is only one question left:
Who is your next?

CHAPTER 8 – END NOTES

1. Keller, T., Chester, T., Montgomery, D., Cosper, M., & Hirsch, A. (2016). *Serving a movement: Doing balanced, gospel-centered ministry in your city.* Zondervan.

2. Strecker, J. (2020). *Church effectiveness: Organizational culture, religioisty, sense of community and civic engagement* [Dissertation].

3. Quinn, R. E. (2004). *Building the bridge as you walk on it: A guide for leading change **(1st edition). Jossey-Bass.***

4. Maxwell, J. C. (2022). *The 21 irrefutable laws of leadership: Follow them and people will follow you* (25th Anniversary edition). HarperCollins Leadership.

5. Wiebe, T. (2024). *What does it mean to follow Jesus?: A clear, biblical picture of discipleship.* Independently published.

ABOUT THE AUTHOR

Dr. James Strecker Jr. has earned a master's degree in organizational leadership and a Ph.D. in Religious and Social Leadership from Omega Graduate School. Dr. Strecker has served over 35 years in church-based ministries developing and coaching disciplemaking programs for students and adults. Through a combination of academic rigor and pastoral care, Dr. Strecker strives to inspire and equip others for effective leadership in their communities. His journey reflects a deep passion for fostering spiritual growth, disciplemaking, and advancing the mission of the church in meaningful ways.

As he continues to lead, coach, and mentor, Dr. Strecker remains dedicated to the principles of Shepherding Leadership, emphasizing the importance of mission, integrity, compassion, and community engagement in all aspects of life.

Dr. Strecker resides in North Platte, NE where he engages in a disciplemaking way of life alongside his wife of 30 years, soon to be college-bound son, daughter serving as a labor and delivery nurse, son-in-law serving as a Deputy Sheriff, parents, family, and friends.

Dr. Strecker serves at Bethel Church in North Platte as an associate pastor, as part of the Evangelical Free Church of America. Dr. Strecker splits his spare time between good BBQ, cycling, and Lego.

LOOKING FOR MORE?

Dr. Strecker regularly posts on his blog at <u>www.</u>
<u>movementmatters.church.</u>

www.Movementmatters.church

www.ingramcontent.com/pod-product-compliance
Lightning Source LLC
Chambersburg PA
CBHW071952100426
42736CB00043B/2830